Spiritual Fathers

Spiritual Fathers

A biblical and practical perspective on spiritual fathers and fathering

Paul Newberry

Sovereign World

Sovereign World Ltd
PO Box 777
Tonbridge
Kent TN11 0ZS
England

Email: info@sovereign-world.com
Website: www.sovereign-world.com

ISBN 1 85240 364 0

Cover design by CCD, www.ccdgroup.co.uk
Typeset by CRB Associates, Reepham, Norfolk
Printed by Clays Ltd, St Ives plc

To my father Jim Newberry

Appreciation

Pat, my wife, has been a constant and cheerful encouragement to me while writing this book – and so have my family. I am grateful also to Tim Pettingale of Sovereign World Publishers who came into my life with friendship and inspiration at a significant time.

Contents

Preface

Honoring My Father – and Fathers

My father was a good and lovely man. His character and reputation has been an ongoing influence and inspiration in my life. "What would Dad do?" is still a consideration when I am making decisions that affect home and family – and I still polish my shoes with him in mind. He held the quaint belief that the state of a man's shoes said something about his character.

My father's commitment to the Lord Jesus Christ was profound and practical. Our family lived on the edge of the New Forest and belonged to a small Pentecostal Mission in the great seaport of Southampton. The life and work of the Mission was central to our everyday life and my personal memories of those early years are all touched with the happiness and joys of what I still call "my home church."

After a heavy day's work at Southampton docks my father would often cycle straight to the mission hall on a Thursday night for the prayer meeting. His public prayers were simple, direct, and loud. Before the "gospel service" on Sunday evenings the people gathering in the hall knew that "the men" were praying in the room at the back – my father and Eddie Irish made sure of that. Prayer, volume, and being Pentecostal were all of a piece to my father. He was sometimes asked to sing a solo in the Sunday night meeting. It was always the same song, "If you've had a kindness shown, pass it on." Sometimes I can still hear, and see him, singing it.

I never ever heard him criticize anyone. It is a quality that I wish I had learned from him to greater effect. Sometimes I feel ashamed, even now, when I recall his straightforward kindliness.

He disciplined my two brothers and me quite naturally. He knew what was required. A book on how to do "parenting" would have seemed very strange to him. He read very little anyway, just his Bible and the *Daily Mirror* (though I can't see him reading today's editions). Disobedience was always serious, usually followed by a stinging sensation on the back of the legs – made worse by short trousers. "I'll tell your father when he gets home" was Mother's last resort. It usually worked.

He loved anything in the nature of a party – and Christmas was the joy of his heart. Boxing Day evening was always filled with friends and fun and food, followed by songs and hilarious games. How cheerful he was and how he enjoyed life.

Even as a boy I knew that people loved and respected Dad. They called him Gentleman Jim. There are only a handful of people left today who knew him. When I see them they some-times say, "You are so much like your father." I know they mean in looks but very little fills me with greater pleasure and pride. A pastor paid tribute to him at his funeral concluding with, "Strong churches are built with men like Jim Newberry." A few weeks back, on a wet and blustery morning at Blackley Cemetery in Manchester, I stood at his and Mother's grave and realized afresh the ongoing influence of his life.

Two men were father-like to me as a young Christian. Winston Shearing was pastor of the Southampton Pentecostal Mission, a man of gentle modesty, infectious humor, and the burning heart of an evangelist (his crusade in Belfast in the early 1950s had wide and lasting effect). By virtue of his gracious character and lovely voice he was a superb leader of a meeting and his masterly "touch" still inspires me.

Don Cox was the teaching elder in the Southampton Mission. It was from him that I first began to understand the atonement, the return of the Lord Jesus Christ (one coming, not two), and baptism in the Spirit. There was much more in that Sunday afternoon Bible class (we were at the Mission all day on Sundays; three gatherings, and an open air service), including sidelights on Charles Haddon Spurgeon, Alexander McClaren and Henry Grattan Guinness. Don Cox has been a remarkable lifelong father-teacher to the Southampton church and to a number of leaders and churches in that area. I honor him and owe him a very great debt.

In later years a number of spiritual fathers touched my life. Donald Gee, Principal of Kenley Bible School during my time as a student, was, while being a spiritual statesman of world renown, faithful in his personal counsel to me. He was thought by some to be distant and aloof but I never found him so.

Alfred Missen made a long journey to our home in Manchester to see me for no reason other than to speak some serious words of concern and admonition into my life. He was led by the Lord to do so and I have never forgotten it.

David Powell, a unique character and father extraordinary to many church leaders, touched my life in various ways over a number of years. On more than one occasion he rang my home very early in the morning to ask if I was out of bed and praying. He usually spoke to my wife Pat. "Are you up before that husband of yours?" he would rumble. "Well, my dear, what's the matter with him? If I were married to you I would be ruling the world by now!" Who could ever forget David's attention? I preached one Sunday at the Rotherham church when he was at the height of his powers and the church was overflowing with spiritual life. I had been speaking for perhaps twenty minutes when he stood up and said, "You've finished. Sit down." He then addressed the great crowd, pointing to a man and his wife and children. "You've been coming long enough," he said. "It's time you repented and believed on Christ. Come forward." The man and his family came and knelt at the front. It was a breathless moment. And he was right, I had finished.

Local church elders, while being overseers, are sometimes spiritual fathers too. This has been the case in the two churches I have served. I owe a great debt to Edmund Rainsbury, an elder and spiritual father of Sharon Tabernacle in Manchester during all our years there. A zealous witness, full of praise and faithful integrity, his care and counsel toward me was personal and profound. And lastly, for over twenty-two years at Manna Christian Fellowship in Maidstone, two elders have had a fatherly concern for my life and ministry. Alf Pitt and Martin Frost have honored me with love, counsel, admonition, and loyalty. Always spiritual but never heavy, straightforward but always kind, I honor them as spiritual fathers and thank God for them.

Chapter 1

Missing Fathers

In Parliament, the seat of British government, fatherhood is traditionally and continually honored. There is a place in the House of Commons reserved, by general acknowledgement and consent, for the "father of the House." The position, occupied at present by Tam Dalyell, is one of respect for maturity and long service, but also carries with it a recognition of knowledge and wisdom, with honor and deference for a certain kind of bearing that is unmistakable while difficult to define – a mixture of integrity, uprightness, maturity, and firm but kindly benevolence. The parliamentary honor is a public and positive recognition that every "house" requires a father, a man of responsibility, stability, and stature.

Early church history has both its apostolic fathers – those who were thought to have known the apostles of Christ – and its early church fathers, significant Christian leaders of the second, third, and fourth centuries.

You will still, sometimes, hear people talk of the "founding fathers" of a movement or institution. In the United States, for instance, the men who signed the original Declaration of Independence are spoken of as the fathers of the nation.

In today's western culture such expressions – father of the house, founding fathers, father-figure – while certainly used, would, I think, be thought slightly quaint and a little out of date. A "progressive" and liberal minority in contemporary western culture (vocal and influential beyond its size) would view the honoring of fathers and fatherhood as a traditional expression of deference belonging to a bygone age.

"Mentor" and "mentoring," words linked with "father" and "fathering" (similar though not entirely synonymous), are more commonly accepted and their reappearance in the field of social care and education is worth noting. It is evidence that some fundamental aspects of mentoring continue to be recognized and valued. A mentor guides and advises, watches over us and provides counsel. Mentor, a figure from Greek mythology, was a friend of Odysseus and guardian and counselor to his son. Modern use of the word "mentor" has elaborated the original idea considerably. A teacher or master is more scholastic and less personal. To be mentored is to have someone who cares about you and your life and takes a consistent interest in your welfare and progress. A mentor's wisdom, maturity, and guidance becomes valuable to you, and their admonition, even discipline, is accepted because the relationship between you is one of honor and esteem.[1]

Though fathers and father figures may not be recognized so much as mentors in contemporary western society, this would be much less true in some eastern cultures. There the honoring of fatherhood and the concept of mentoring is more widely acknowledged and accepted. Mr Myagi in the film *The Karate Kid* is a good example. He is an older oriental who becomes a mentor and father-like friend to the young Daniel, whom he calls "Danielson." The young man's fondness and respect for the old man grows until he is willing to accept discipline as well as instruction as an expression of care and affection.

Decrease in natural understanding

In western society as it stands at present there is a serious lack of understanding regarding fathers and fathering. Some observers would view this as the result of a deliberate attack on family life and relationships. They see a concerted policy by humanist groups to question and discard "outmoded conventions" such as husband and wife marriage, and father and mother family. If this *is* happening (and there is evidence that it is) we need look no further for at least one major reason why fathers have become itinerant, and why recent generations are suffering for lack of them.

Lynda Lee Potter wrote in the *Daily Mail*,

"We've come close in recent years to saying that fathers don't matter, fathers aren't necessary and mothers and fathers are interchangeable. We see the disastrous results in our prisons and reform centres where more than 75% of the inmates come from homes where there are no fathers. Boys in particular need male influence to demonstrate that you can be strong but compassionate and that being gentle doesn't mean you are a coward."[2]

The decrease in natural understanding regarding fathers is one of a number of problems connected with the increase in mother-based one-parent families. A disturbing percentage of children are growing up with no practical experience of a loving respons-ible father. This means, alongside all the more immediate social and emotional difficulties created by lack of fatherhood, that the natural framework of father and family in which God has chosen to reveal Himself to us in Scripture is diminished. Consequently a vital element fundamental to our understanding of God is seriously impaired.

Not only is "father" an empty word for many children, it is already an irrelevant word to many young adults. The father-hood of God, therefore, carries little meaning (or a distorted meaning) for increasing numbers of people. Further decline in this direction will view fatherhood not simply as unfashionable but as optional, a "component" of life to be discarded if considered unnecessary.

Thinking positively about fatherhood

In spite of all this, natural fatherhood cries out in every genera-tion for a clear framework of truth in which to define itself. In the present generation the need is crucial. The current situation means that many young men lack positive models of father-hood. Their experience of fathering is unhappy or unhealthy and the fatherhood of God as the major framework for thinking positively about fatherhood is foreign and strange to them. In the contemporary mind (both male and female) fatherhood is too readily reduced to the capacity for reproduction. While this, obviously, is fundamental to natural fatherhood there are ele-ments essentially connected with the reproductive faculty with-out which fatherhood becomes a mere biological ability.

For example, willingness to accept and take responsibility is a necessary element in fatherhood. It is elemental both to my capacity for reproduction and the attitude I adopt to what I reproduce; because I am *able* to bring into being I must take responsibility for *what* I bring into being. Further, my attitude to what I reproduce should be one of ownership and stewardship. I cannot avoid this responsibility. Many men who father children casually often, and unexpectedly, find themselves overwhelmed with unfamiliar feelings of accountability and concern – "I should do something about this, but what?"; "I can't just walk away, this is my child." Post-modern thinking provides no cohesive framework whatsoever for such feelings of accountability. The contemporary mind has been subdued into nonresponsibility. We are no longer creatures of free will making decisions for which we are accountable; any thought of being held responsible for personal moral choice is viewed with suspicion. The criteria for assessing behavior are no longer "Is it right?" but "Is it harming anyone?"; no longer "Is it wrong?", but "How many people are doing it?" "Willfully single mothers, nomadic or peripatetic fathers" must not have responsibility assigned to them.[3] A true and proper view of human being, however, of free will and accountability, affirms feelings of responsibility and concern; it restores honor and esteem to fathers and raises fatherhood to a position of dignity, respect, and fulfillment.

Fathers and authority

Fatherhood also carries authority. The caricature of the austere, distant "Victorian" tyrant has been used to denigrate the responsible and kindly father taking his place at the head of the family, carrying influence and bearing authority. An unpopular view? Yes, certainly, but not wrong for that reason. The endemic loss of respect for authority at all levels of life in the western world has developed hand in hand with the elevation of individualism, the loss of true community, and the rise of feminism.[4] Individualism has, among other things, made "me" (and my "private morality") the center of the universe and therefore constituted objective and absolute standards and requirements a hindrance to any expression of my personal liberty. The loss of true community suffers as a result of such institutional selfishness, and those called or appointed to administrate the standards and requirements recognized as necessary for true community to function are viewed negatively as servants of repression. Feminism has been one of the stronger dogmas used as a flagship in the battle to belittle "conventions" deemed oppressive to individual freedom such as marriage and family. It is not difficult to see, therefore, how fathers, who carry headship, responsibility and authority, have been marginalized and fathering robbed of honor, deference, and respect. Law, authority, and obedience are fundamental to righteousness and therefore essential to universal happiness. Paternal responsibility, both divine and human, is necessarily connected to its administration.

With all that we are saying about fathers and fathering, we will become conscious, as we approach the source and heart of it, that a prevailing element informs and infuses all else. That element, quite simply and profoundly, is love. Because God is our Father and God is love, fathering and love are essentially and inextricably bound together. We will return to this again in a later chapter because it is so central to our theme, but let us at least say here that the sense of responsibility inherent in fatherhood is supported by a foundation of affection and care. Strong men will melt with tender devotion over their daughters and look with loving pride upon their sons. They will protect and defend them like warriors, often surprised at the depth of their own feelings. Fatherhood is a well of love and responsibility, of authority, protection, and guidance, all crucial factors in the development, stability, and fulfillment of a life. If the well runs dry the quality of life is inevitably affected.

It is surely not a coincidence that the current call from journalists (often "secular prophets"), the caring professions and educational and social specialists for fathers and fatherhood to be viewed more positively, is making itself heard alongside a desire increasingly expressed among church leaders and churches for spiritual fathers.

Part of the Christian contribution to this resurgence of concern, both natural and spiritual, must be a vigorous exposition and application of the biblical perspective on fatherhood. We must rise to the task, approach it with prayer and confidence, and take pains to do it well. For one thing we cannot afford to see fathering categorized as yet another method for church "success," another growth technique or "spiritual" therapy. We must locate our thinking about it in the framework of divine revelation, receiving it as a profound doctrine filled with biblical content and contemporary relevance.

The father theme runs like a country road through Scripture; we need to take the road and appreciate the journey. Speed is not always necessary or helpful to our spiritual progress; we may well be missing fatherhood, both as an understanding and as a ministry in the modern church, because we have taken the religious motorway. High velocity Christianity too often fails to appreciate the grace and width of God's country for the flash of the dual carriageway. At some point we will have to slow down. Fathers are rarely in a rush.

Notes

1. This may become true of some teachers and masters where the relationship develops a personal note; they would then become more like mentors and perhaps even fathers.
2. In an article published in 2000. I quote Lynda Lee Potter as an illustration of responsible journalism committed generally to the natural and moral order of father and mother family and parenthood. Her opinions are open to debate and her statistics to verification.
3. Harry Blamires, *The Post-Christian Mind* (SPCK, 2001), p. 46.
4. The twentieth-century movement for the liberation of women from domination and repression, while sharing some of the distinctives of feminism, should not be confused with it. Feminism is a philosophy committed to the "equal" headship and authority of women.

Chapter 2

Fatherhood and God

This is not, specifically, a book on doctrine. Nevertheless, the foundations of Christian believing and behaving are inescapably doctrinal, and doctrine, for all its bad press, is the age-long and dynamic bedrock upon which our thinking and living is built. We must not judge the authority and creative energy of God's word by the dry and perfunctory way in which it is sometimes handled.

If we are to understand anything about spiritual fathers and fathering we must begin by looking carefully at God and His Son the Lord Jesus Christ. Fatherhood has its origin in God; Scripture reveals that He is the "ground" from which it springs. When we think upon God we are coming face to face with fatherhood at its source. There is, therefore, some doctrine in this chapter. You will find it in other chapters too. We must do as the apostle Paul – spiritual father to the young leader Titus, *"my true son in our common faith"* (Titus 1:4) – instructed, and *"teach what is in accord with sound doctrine"* (Titus 2:1).

Ephesians 3:14–15

In this passage Paul states,

> *"For this reason I kneel before the Father, from whom his whole family in heaven and on earth derives its name. I pray that out of his glorious riches he may strengthen you with power through his Spirit in your inner being, so that Christ may dwell in your hearts through faith. And I pray that you, being rooted and established in love, may have power, together with all the saints, to grasp how wide and long and high and deep is the love of Christ, and to*

*know this love that surpasses knowledge – that you may be filled
to the measure of all the fullness of God."*

(Ephesians 3:14–19)

I've quoted the whole passage because it seems to me that here is
as clear a definition of fathering as we could ask for.

- A father will strengthen us in our "inner being" out of the
  riches of his own life and by the power of his own spirit.

- He will focus on Christ and His dwelling in our hearts,
  encouraging us to make Him the center of our affections.

- He will be concerned for our private spiritual reality and
  security, helping us to maintain a strong and healthy root
  system that draws upon divine love, grasping something of
  its dimensions and profoundly affected by its nature.

- A true spiritual father will serve the interests of our inner
  life, seeking to ensure that there is a measure of God's
  fullness in us. He will be like this whether fathering a
  church, a team, or an individual, the rich depths in his
  own life being a source for the establishing of ours.

At the start of the passage Paul says, *"I kneel before the Father."*
That has to be the position of acknowledgement and honor in
which we are most likely to receive a father's ministry. Recognition and acceptance of a spiritual father, a submissive spirit
toward him and a desire to be cared for, guided and loved: all this
will make us amenable to a father's interest and concern.

Fathers in the Old Testament

Our understanding will be further helped if we appreciate that
this profound statement made by Paul to the Ephesians has its
roots in the Hebrew view of fathers and fatherhood contained
in the Old Testament. Hebrew social structures were patriarchal,
the father was head of the family and of the household. He was
given honor and respect, which he shared with his wife, while
taking upon himself the numerous responsibilities necessary to
the order, government, and blessing of his family. The father
provided for them, meeting the various needs of his household
by his diligent ordering of family employment and the wise use

of resources, and arranging for the prudent management of finance. The Hebrew father's responsibility as a provider, therefore, reflected God's provision for His creation (Genesis 1:29; 2:9):

> *"You open your hand*
> *and satisfy the desires of every living thing."*   (Psalm 145:16)

He is *"Our Father in heaven"* who gives us each day our daily bread. Fatherhood, both natural and spiritual, replicates the loving and responsible provision of God for His children.

So the New Testament promise completes the Old Testament picture and declares, *"My God will meet all your needs ..."* (Philippians 4:19). Why? Because He is a faithful Father who delights to fulfill His paternal responsibility toward us. He does so by common grace for the whole of creation, and by special grace for His chosen people *"according to His glorious riches in Christ Jesus."* We are therefore enriched and blessed in order to be a blessing both to one another and to the world around us. Election to the Father's family and the Father's blessing is always to this end, that He through blessing us might, through us, bless the rest of humankind. Election and blessing is never for a lesser but always for a larger end.

The Hebrew father was not only the family provider, he was also the family protector. Job cried out regarding his faithful fatherhood,

> *"I was a father to the needy;*
> *I took up the case of the stranger."*   (Job 29:16)

In so doing, such fathers were following the example of God,

> *"A father to the fatherless, a defender of widows,*
> *is God in his holy dwelling."*   (Psalm 68:5)

The father watched over his family, including his extended family, to ensure that no one took advantage of any member, especially the widows and the orphans. Those with no father were seriously "at risk." Again the prayer that Jesus taught us takes up the Old Testament picture of the protecting father and

directs us to *"Our Father, who art in heaven,"* reminding us that to
be fatherless is to have no protector, to be undefended, to be lost.

One of the most wonderful, but sometimes neglected, doctrines is that of adoption. We have received *"the adoption of
sons,"* says Paul (Galatians 4:5 KJV), and been made heirs of God
and joint heirs with Christ. It is, however, a New Testament
doctrine (legal adoption was peculiarly Roman not Hebrew),
though the idea is present in the Old Testament in God "adopting" Israel as His "son" and thereby revealing His Fatherhood.

In addition, the Hebrew father, as head of the family, was
responsible for its spiritual instruction. God manifested through
such a faithful father a revelation of Himself so that the earthly
father, by both his position and his teaching, expressed the
divine nature and order. The Hebrew father in this respect was
priest in his household, standing before God for them and before
them for God. A father's authority represented the law of the
Lord and his teaching enabled them to walk in the light. It was
on this basis that the family worshiped. Central to the father's
instruction and the family worship was the Passover ceremony
rehearsed each year to commemorate their deliverance as God's
people from the slavery and death of Egypt. The father was told,

> *"And when your children ask you, 'What does this ceremony
> mean to you?' then tell them, 'It is the Passover sacrifice to the
> Lord ... ' "*   (Exodus 12:26–27)

and,

> *"In days to come when your son asks you, 'What does this mean?'
> say to him, 'With a mighty hand the Lord brought us out of
> Egypt, out of the land of slavery ... ' "*   (Exodus 13:14)

This commemoration was, and still is, celebrated by the father
in Hebrew families. Because of Christ, the "Lamb of God,"
sacrificed for us once for all, the Old Testament Passover finds
its fullness in the New Testament communion of the body
and blood of Christ, celebrated now by the people of God and
administrated by gift-ministries bestowed by Christ Himself.

The Old Testament father then was at once a provider, a
protector, and a teacher; he represented God Himself as head of
the family and household, upheld the law of the Lord, celebrated

His mighty acts and instructed his children and family in the meaning of those acts. He was responsible in all these ways for his offspring.

The source of all fatherhood

This Old Testament fatherhood pattern and function stands as part of the historic revelation of the person and action of God. And it stands again as the divinely revealed backdrop for those New Testament statements regarding all natural and spiritual fatherhood and fathering. We return to say, then, that God Himself is the source of all fatherhood and fathering and of all our fundamental understanding of it.

It is necessary to emphasize that the fatherhood of God does not in any way depend upon His adopting us through grace to be His sons. He is not Father because we are His children, He is essentially and eternally Father because He is *"the God and Father of our Lord Jesus Christ"* (Romans 15:6; 2 Corinthians 1:3; Ephesians 1:3): "Therefore He is the archetypal Father, the source of Fatherhood, the Father from whom all Fatherhood in heaven and on earth is named."[1]

It is this essential revelation of the fatherhood of God that forms the foundation for our consideration of fatherhood and mentoring, both natural and spiritual. If we begin anywhere else other than God we are liable to locate our thinking in the contemporary, and shifting, ideas of the time and culture in which we live. Always, in all Christian ministry, our fundamental frame of reference must be *"In the beginning God ... "* (Genesis 1:1), rather than "in the beginning society," or "in the beginning biology, or philosophy or psychiatry ... "

Note
1. Alan Richardson, *An Introduction to the Theology of the New Testament* (SCM Press Ltd, 1972), p. 264.

Chapter 3

Christ and His Father

We must resist the thought that fatherhood is a minor idea supplying sidelights on a particular type of Christian ministry. In the life of the Lord Jesus Christ, His Father and His Father's business was all that He was about. We cannot attach to our own father-relationships, either natural or spiritual, a similar kind of consecration to that existing between the Lord Jesus Christ and His Father in heaven; there were and are elements in that relationship beyond application to ourselves. Nevertheless, we may accept that fatherhood stands closer to the life and ministry of the church and its leaders than might be supposed. That much, at the very least, may be understood from the relationship of the Lord Jesus Christ with His Father. Nowhere are these things so clearly revealed and demonstrated than in that relationship: from the beginning Jesus lived, spoke, and worked in union with the Father. It was in the light of this understanding, in its reality and experience, that He saw Himself as Son and Servant, a personal perception that was fundamental to all that He said and did.

"My Father's business"

Before looking at this in more detail consider the following episodes in the life of Christ that give immediate indications of this far-reaching truth.

When He went missing on a journey from Jerusalem to Nazareth and was eventually discovered by his anxious parents in the temple, Jesus, even as a young boy, answered their questions with one of his own, a remarkable question in the circumstances: *"Didn't you know I had to be in my Father's house?"*

(Luke 2:49). At twelve years of age His relationship to His Father and to His Father's "house" (translated "business" in the Authorized Version) was already becoming a major influence in His life and thinking.

Later the Father's "business" would become the touchstone of His life, His baptism the public acceptance of the message and mission upon which He had been sent. It was His Father's voice at that decisive moment, together with the fullness of the Spirit's power, that released Him into His public ministry:

> *"And a voice from heaven said, 'This is my Son, whom I love; with him I am well pleased.'"*   (Matthew 3:17)

From that moment His every word and work was a willing and loving expression of His Father's will. For the first time since the heart-rending rebellion of Adam, the Father could look upon a man and say, *"This is my Son ... I am well pleased."* To be sure there were, in the long years of the Old Testament, many in whom, in His astounding patience, the Father took pleasure. But it was all in the love light of the One who was to come, *"the One and Only, who is at the Father's side ... has made him known"* (John 1:18).

When asked by His disciples for some instruction on prayer Jesus began with, *"Father, hallowed be your name ... "* (Luke 11:2). When asked by skeptical teachers for authentication of His identity and mission Jesus referred them directly to the Father:

> *"I have testimony weightier than that of John* [the Baptist]. *For the very work that the Father has given me to finish, and which I am doing, testifies that the Father has sent me. And the Father who sent me has himself testified concerning me."*
>
>   (John 5:36–37)

Jesus would eventually declare, to the blinkered astonishment and anger of the religious hierarchy, *"I and the Father are one"* (John 10:30). In due course the Father's "business" would inevitably take Him down into overwhelming sorrow of mind and heart – *"My Father, if it is possible, may this cup be taken from me ... "* (Matthew 26:39) – and into death, *"even death on a cross"* (Philippians 2:8), because He made Himself a ready and obedient

captive to a will beyond His own: *"not my will, but yours be done"*
(Luke 22:42).

The dominating note, therefore, in the life of Christ and the
consuming passion of His heart was, and is, loving submission
and obedience to the will of the Father, and it is not too much to
say that the age-long happiness of the entire universe depended
upon it.

> *"... he was heard because of his reverent submission. Although
> he was a Son, he learned obedience from what he suffered and,
> once made perfect, he became the source of eternal salvation for
> all who obey him ..."*   (Hebrews 5:7–9)

All the exhaustless glory of salvation has its origins, not in a
triumph of independent individualism, but in the endless love of
the Father for the Son and the endless love of the Son for His
Father, tested out and proved to the last degree in His mission as
Son of man. The exultant ministry of God the Holy Spirit speaks,
now, the wonders of such love into the hearts of men and
women and will continue to do so until the light dawns and the
sin shadows of the long night give way to the radiance of day and
all hearts see the truth at last, for it is said that *"love never fails"*
(1 Corinthians 13:8).

Christ both Son and Servant

We need to go a little further. Two aspects of Christ's life and
ministry stand central to the New Testament: they are the
fatherhood of God and the kingdom of God. Both are present
in the Old Testament but come to a fullness of revelation in the
New Testament in the person and teaching of Jesus.

The calm but insistent emphasis in the teaching of Christ
upon God as Father is recorded in the Gospel of John. His
identity and mission is authenticated again and again in these
compelling passages where He teaches a unique and inimitable
relationship with the Father. This teaching became the historic
reason for His arrest and reached its unavoidable consequence, as
already seen, in His death on the cross.

The presence and power of the kingdom of God was revealed
by Christ in similar fashion, first by virtue of what He was –
the servant of the Lord and of His kingdom – and then, within

that framework of unique service, by His specific kingdom teaching.

Both of these primary and immense themes were revealed and manifested personally by what Christ was, the Father's unique Son and the kingdom's true Servant, and then declared specifically in His preaching and teaching. Hence His teaching ministry was an extension of the revelation of His person. He was, and is, the Word of God incarnate, the truth of God in human form. He was *"found in appearance as a man"* (Philippians 2:8), both Son and Servant of God. There could be no greater revelation of the Father than that manifested and declared by the Father's one and only Son, He *"who is at the Father's side has made him known"* (John 1:18). In *"taking the very nature of a servant"* (Philippians 2:7), the Son of God became the servant of God to reveal the kingdom of God. The kingdom of God comes where the will of God is done. Hence the life of Jesus the Son, lived in perfect obedience to the Father's will, manifested the Father's kingdom and inaugurated its reign on earth as a new dynamic of life – new, at least, among fallen humankind.

In doing this Christ brought eternal light to bear upon the center and focus of all the ages, His Father, the one true living God, and His kingdom rule. By loving obedience to His Father's will He made it possible, in and through His death and resurrection, for us to be born again, and, by that new birth to see God's kingdom for ourselves; to pray for its coming, to begin to seek its interests beyond all else, and to come to know and understand the wonder of our Father – a wonder that always leads to worship and to witness.

All ideas of fatherhood, therefore, are to do with the realization of our identity as both sons and servants in relation to the Father: sons to speak the truth about His person and character (God really is loving),[1] and servants to seek and serve His kingdom interests. Fatherly care, counsel, and discipline, therefore, even when being applied to untidy and unhappy church problems or difficult personal circumstances must take place in this larger framework, and for greater blessing than the resolving of immediate difficulties. Or at least the resolving of difficulties must be seen as part of a much greater and more enduring glory. If we have some understanding of the divine origins of fatherhood, spiritual mentoring will not dissolve into yet another leadership technique, to have its day as one more means of temporary success. We will value it for what it is, an essential element in the ongoing life and future ministry of the family of God, and receive it as preparation for service in God's eternal scheme of things. This must, to some degree, have been in the mind of the writer to the Hebrews when he said, *"God disciplines us for our good, that we may share in His holiness"* (Hebrews 12:10).

The Father's glory in the Son

Christ's life in all its varied aspects is a fulfillment of Old Testament promise and prophecy. All the historic revelation of God comes to its fullness in Him: He is the sum and substance of every Old Testament type, picture, and figure. But more even than this. There is in His life and ministry a revelation and a manifestation of God that touches all other truth. God, as we have seen, is certainly revealed in the Old Testament as Father. The framework of that revelation, however, is national and ethnic. In Christ that framework is confirmed but measurelessly widened. God is the God of Israel, the One who chooses Israel as His special treasure, who calls Israel "His son." It is through the Israel "son" that the incarnate Son came to reveal *"the God and Father from whom all fatherhood derives its name,"* the universal Father. That revelation came in all its fullness with the Lord Jesus Christ. He is the "Word of the Father," His final and complete revelation. God, in these last days, has spoken to us Son-wise. Christ Jesus is *"the radiance of God's glory and the exact representation of His being"* (Hebrews 1:3). This is why He could say, *"If you knew me, you would know my Father also"* (John 8:19). Fathering and sonship, then, is more than another idea. It has its origin, and shares by spiritual union, in the relationship between God the Father and God the Son and, because of that, will carry in it elements of divine revelation. A true spiritual father will minister out of his relationship with God. That relationship, constituting him a son, will in its turn enable him to love and serve his own "sons in the faith."

Fathering out of spiritual union

My relationship with my natural son has taught me many things, probably more than I have taught him. In seeking to love and guide him I have found myself constantly thinking back into my understanding of the relationship I have with God. His grace has been the reservoir from which I've drawn, His law the script from which I've sought to teach, His love the light by which I've tried to walk. In that sense my son, while hardly knowing it, has been touched by the Father within and beyond me. My attitude, counsel, sanctions and example have been a flawed and faint reflection of His love, grace, and authority. This may, in one sense, be said of all true fathering.

When we turn to consider in later chapters more practical aspects of fatherhood and mentoring we will have to remember that beneath the various ideas and concepts that lie so readily on the surface there swells the boundless ocean of our Father God Himself. If we will remember this and think on it spiritual fathering will become a manifestation of His life rather than the mere application of mentoring skills. There is always room, of course, for natural wisdom and common sense, but there is a higher and deeper level of ministry. Its origins lie in the truth and doctrine of spiritual union, the oneness of spirit that we have with God the Father through our Lord Jesus Christ, that is the source of our life and ministry:

> *"This is what we speak, not in words taught us by human wisdom but in words taught by the Spirit, expressing spiritual truths in spiritual words."* (1 Corinthians 2:13)

Spiritual fathering must serve from this divine source if it is to quicken and nourish the life and call of God in a spiritual son or a church family.

We live at a time when religious advice and charismatic counsel is promoted in so many forms. From mega super-store Christianity through unaccountable preaching positivists to a thousand peculiar quacks comes "guidance" and inspiration, often at a price and "gift" wrapped, but there is, I think, a lack of cohesive biblical exposition and divine illumination at local church level. The trend may be reversed, or at least counteracted, not by retreat into hidebound fundamental evangelicalism, an over emphasis on social concern or a migration across tracks into a new liturgical quietism (elements of which might be welcome), but by renewed appreciation of a high view of Scripture with a rediscovery of the nature and being of God that is both doctrinal and devotional. Truly *"the fear of the Lord is the beginning of wisdom ... "* (Psalm 110:10).

Note
1. Confronting, with the truth, the lies spread by the devil regarding Him, a fundamental element of our witness to "the gospel of God."

Chapter 4

Fathers – and Love

"The world was made by a Lover, it was made for love, and it will only work when all men love again."   (John Phillips)

We have said that love and responsibility are two elements fundamental to fathers and fathering. We must look a little further now at love. If the fatherhood of God forms for us the ground and framework upon which and within which we are to discover the root and reality of spiritual fathering, then any revelation of the nature of God is crucial – and God is love.[1]

By this is meant at least, among more truth about God than we can presently know, that love is defined by His nature and disposition. Love has no existence "by itself," it is an essential element of His being and therefore qualified by all else that He reveals Himself to be. God is eternal, then so is His love; He is holy, then so is His love; He is infinite, then so, again, is His love. Equally all His will, purpose and action is an expression of love because, again, that is what He is.

Such a definition of divine love is not always easy to accept or understand especially against the background of an Old Testament narrative in which God appears at times to command violence and cruelty. It presents a similar difficulty as a Christian world view or philosophy of existence and history – so much appears to be anything but love. Part of the problem here is that we tend to read *our* idea of love back into God. On the basis of how we think love should act we say, "God wouldn't do that" or "I can't believe in a God who allows that." But we are fallen and our ideas of love are fallen too. Because of this it is exceedingly hard for us to define love, or come to terms with what appear to us to be negative expressions of it. We may reluctantly accept that *"the Lord disciplines those He loves"* and understand the need for endurance under discipline *"For what son is not disciplined by his father?"* (see Hebrews 12:5–11). In these instances we use expressions such as "tough love" when thinking of short-term discipline and hardship. But long-term suffering is much more difficult.

Our tendency is to reduce definitions of love to a romantic feeling or an uncontrollable passion, and use them to justify any relationship we might happen to desire: "I can't help it, I'm in love" or "I know you think it wrong, but we are in love." It is only as we come back to the revelation that God gives of Himself in Scripture that we begin to glimpse love at its source and in reality. The great statements of Scripture by which God reveals Himself are always within the framework and against the background of His dealings with us, of His actions in history. Because God is love many of these actions are inscrutable. It is when we come to the New Testament record, however, to God "fulfilling" all the promises and pictures of the Old Testament by sending His Son into the world to die at our hands in order to redeem us from sin and death, that the enigma of divine love reaches its pinnacle. Here it is said that *"God so loved the world that He gave His one and only Son"* (John 3:16), and that in His Son's death in our place upon the cross – *"while we were still sinners"* – God is actually commending and demonstrating His love toward us (Romans 5:8). Here, in violent, cruel torture and death, is revealed and manifested the very nature of God. In Christ's dying God is saying, "This is what I am like, this is love."

The enigma of divine love

It is as we look at the cross, as we "survey it" as Isaac Watts said in his great hymn, that the vast age-long enigma of love and suffering begins, slowly, to unfold. Here, in the cross, the revelation "God is love" comes to its full and final expression in the saving act of God in Christ. It is in contemplation of the doctrine – for that is how we "survey" and gaze upon the cross – that the reality of it dawns upon us, that is how our minds and hearts apprehend glimpses of its truth. We must not, of course, take this to mean that narrative and doctrine is for us the fullness of spiritual life. The preaching of the gospel, with all its theology, will bring us to the cross, but then it may leave us to gaze, as God the Holy Spirit lifts for us the curtain and shows us, in the pain of God the Son, the suffering of God the Father. The cross and what it means, its doctrine, is a revelation of the one true and living God: *He* is our vision, our "Father in heaven . . . ". Doctrine is the journey, He is the destination. Receiving, knowing, and understanding Him – and that can only, now, be in some minute measure – will awaken and amaze the mind and heart and eventually bring eternal life to the broken spirit – and to a broken world.

> "By the cross of Jesus standing,
> Love our straitened souls expanding,
> Taste we now the peace and grace,
> Health from yonder tree is flowing,
> Heavenly light is on it glowing,
> From the blessed Sufferer's face."[2]

Here, in the cross, is the love of God, love beyond all selfish desire and compulsive craving, all personal gratification or possessive control. Doctrine and sacrament must stand hand in hand at the cross and serve together through the church to bring us continually before Christ's sacrifice so that we might be faced with and look upon a "love that passes all understanding." Here we may catch a glimpse of an almost dazzling ray of light from a far-off age when everything in all the created universe is in harmonious accord under the benevolent headship of Christ, when all authority and rule is love, when Father, Son and Spirit, with all creation, are as one to the praise of His glory. An age beyond when the love of God in and through the cross of Christ will have conquered every mind and heart, and the irresistible reign of sovereign love has brought all His enemies under His feet and shown ultimately that God's word is true, love cannot fail.

The love and the law of the Lord

Through the cross, where we face the Father's anguish in giving His Son to the law of sin and death, we may look back over the Old Testament. It is in the light of the cross that we interpret the "acts" of God that may seem to us so terrible. All the law of the Lord in the Old Testament, inexorable, just and true,

working itself out in the gloom of days unlit by the Light of the
world, came to its full and final expression in the death of Christ
upon the cross. And then we see, in that terrible "act," that the
Father's love and the Father's law are demonstrated together
to be righteous, His love is holy love. It fulfills through the
obedience of His Son all the law's demands so that the Holy
Spirit can testify in the court of every believer's heart to the
eternal satisfaction and efficacy of the cross.

If we are to see the Father's love in truth we must see it in this
way, in the cross, where the law is satisfied. The tendency, if
we do not, is to sentimentalize the love of God and see it as
something that circumnavigates judgment and justice, as a
mercy that "lets us off." This would strike at the very heart of
the gospel for a love that takes no account of the law of the Lord
cannot be the love of God, and could therefore make no
satisfaction for sin in the death of Christ. We would be left to
an illegitimate mercy – and eternal despair. The mercy we receive
is securely founded upon the law of the Lord being satisfied by
the obedience of Christ in our stead. That obedience was an
eternal demonstration of love divine, of the Father's holy and
righteous love.

To divorce the Father's love and the Father's law will lead us to
believe that a father's love in any instance has nothing to do
with any form of order, rule, discipline or punishment. Such a
divorce would in fact support (and may in fact already be
responsible for) the contemporary doctrines of "free expression," "no restraint," and "individual liberty" that bring such
havoc to marriage, family, community and society.

The Father's love and fathering

All fathering is a manifestation of love. It has its origins in God
the Father Himself, and may, at the last, bring us home to Him.
Spiritual fathers will always be "expressions" of God's love, love
that is both free and full of grace because it delights to keep the
law of the Lord, love that keeps no record of wrongs, love that
rebukes and chastens, love that is longsuffering and kind – kind
enough to allow suffering, both to fathers as well as children.

Whatever the full meaning of the parable of the prodigal son
proves to be, it shows at least that the father's heart ached as
much as the son's shame eventually burned. It took him to the

door again and again to strain his eyes for a glimpse of his son coming home. Fathers get hurt because they love, and sometimes they hurt for a long time – but the prodigal's father rejoiced at the last. There was delight and celebration. The parable teaches that the long low days of waiting and hoping ended not in despair but in joy.

The ages through which a rebellious, lost and wandering humankind has squandered its birthright and reached its lowest depths in the darkness of Calvary, will, when those same ages come to their fullness, resound with the high praises of joy and pleasure as He whom the Father sent to bring back the lost returns home, *"bringing many sons to glory"* (Hebrews 2:10).

And there are lights along the dark ages that anticipate the dawn of the coming day. A missionary couple who served God all their lives with faithfulness and sacrifice had "lost" a son in the process. After the long years, and in their "retirement," they received a phone call. It was the son. He had returned to the Lord. I saw the couple at their diamond wedding celebration listen with joy as he sang to them a song of love. I know only too well that this does not happen for everyone in this life. When it does, it is a chorus from a time to come at the consummation of these gospel ages when the Father's family, brought home at the last by His Son, will sing to Him their songs of love.

Love lies beneath all ministry

It is only within this age-long view of the saving purposes of God that the love of His Father heart, with all its anguish and all its pleasures, can be properly considered. Unless there is a destination and a consummation in which all elements of the journey find their true place we will be homeless wanderers forever. In this case all fatherhood and all mentoring will have been as hopeless as unending night. And there are philosophies of hopelessness that combine to condemn us to such desolation, to what Bertrand Russell called "unyielding despair."

Yet the truth is gloriously other than this.

God so loved the world that He gave His Son for the world; in the Father's giving and the Son's dying there is commended by the Spirit's working a love that cannot fail, that triumphs over death and out of that triumph, through resurrection and ascension, ministers not unyielding despair but unending grace. In our Lord Jesus Christ holy love is even now upon the throne of the universe.

The disclosure of the Father's love in the sacrifice of the Son's life is the foundation that lies beneath *all* spiritual ministry. But because the Father's love is the source of all love the ministry of spiritual fathers represents it in a special way. This much is surely true: fathering and spiritual mentoring is not merely the recovery of a spiritual modus operandi, it is the release of an eternal dynamic and the restoration of a divine delight. The substance and content of true fathering is created in communion, in an ongoing contemplation of the love of God commended in the cross of Christ. All of us may seek the reality of such spiritual life of course, but in fathers and their ministry it is brought to us in a singular manner.

> *"And now these three remain: faith, hope, and love. But the greatest of these is love."* (1 Corinthians 13:13)

Notes

1. This is not all that God reveals Himself to be, of course, God is spirit and God is light. It is the relationship between the spirit (breath or life of God), light (truth or law of God), and love that helps us to maintain symmetry of thought regarding God.
2. Horatius Bonar 1808–1889, *Redemption Hymnal* (1960 ed.), No. 175.

Chapter 5

Fathers – and Relationship

Fathers and mothers stand to us in the closest of all natural relationships. We exist because of them. Scripture recognizes the constant and fundamental nature of the relationship by, for example, the repeated expression "was the father of ..." or "the son of" in Jesus' genealogy in Matthew 1 and Luke 3:21–38. The Authorized Version uses the word "begat," emphasizing the essential reproductive element in natural fatherhood and, as we have already seen, placing husbands and fathers at the head of the natural order.

Fatherhood gives significance and placement to all other categories of personal relationship, to mothers, children, grandparents, and extended family. When fathers recognize and accept their divinely defined place and responsibility all others may properly find theirs; when fathers reject or neglect their role others are forced to find function and definition for themselves without reference to the biblical framework. Because rebellion against God is in the nature of sin, all that is of God falls foul of that rebellion. The natural order, being of God, being "born in" us according to the law of the Lord, is therefore subject, often unwittingly, to rebellion, transgression of the law, and inward conflict. Marriage, paternal headship, and family order all suffer more or less from our sinful rebellion and lawlessness. This is a fundamental fact underlying whole areas of social stress and despair, and all sciences seeking to address humankind's plight without taking note of and giving full weight to this crucial data are seriously flawed. God's gracious commission, given in and through the Lord Jesus Christ, to go into all the world and preach the gospel has huge sociological implications.

The following we can state clearly: that God the Father stands as sovereign Lord and head of all things, that there is *"one God and Father of all, who is over all and through all and in all"* (Ephesians 4:6), and that from Him *"his whole family in heaven and on earth derives its name"* (Ephesians 3:15). Both the position and function of fathers have their origin in the position and function of God. The cry for fathers and for fathering comes from an almost unwitting confession of rebellion against the divine order and a longing for the law of the Lord to replace the chaos of sin. Spiritual fathering and mentoring must be rooted in this understanding of God. In fact all spiritual ministry, because it is employed by God the Father to reproduce (beget) and nourish His life in the life of man, must have its root system in the divine order.

The framework of life

Relationships are the framework of life. Both as creatures (we are made by God) and persons (we are made like God), human beings are relational in every category of their existence, spiritual, social, and physical. To be human is to be relational. In this essential and biblical sense human relations are a crucial element in the construction of a sound doctrine of humanity, which, after the doctrine of God, is so sorely needed at the present time, among both Christians and non-Christians alike.

One aspect of relationship, the emphasis on inter-personal relationships in church life, has been given singular prominence over the last thirty years or so, particularly among charismatic evangelicals and "new" churches. Relationships, between leaders and among the people, have been recognized as a central issue. It *is* a vital emphasis and has led to a renewal of reality in fellowship and community and, notwithstanding excesses, to commitment and accountability. Relationship and relating is fundamental; to understand it is to understand ourselves.

We must, however, go on to say more than this. Inter-personal relationships, while necessary, are but one aspect of relationship and relating and the focus on this one aspect has obscured deeper and more essential elements in regard to relationship as a whole that call for examination and understanding. The contemporary tendency has been to think of relationship in just one way, as an attachment or friendship that overtakes us experimentally, a union of feeling to which we give assent and attention for as long as the association is fulfilling for us. This is invariably what is meant today by relationship. Unhappily Christian thinking on relationship has drifted in the same direction.

But this is not the only sense in which relationship is presented to us in Scripture, it is not even the primary sense. The words "relationship," "relational" and "relate" define not only an attachment that we experience, they define a position in which we stand, a position in regard to certain people and institutions. As already said all of us have been born *of* relationship and *into* relationship. We are the offspring of a father and mother and have been born into relationship with them and with others related to them, to brothers, sisters, grandparents, and extended family. These relationships are natural, that is, they are in the nature of our human being. Our recognition of them creates a framework in which natural and moral obligations form a foundation for the development of self-consciousness and other-consciousness, with respect, honor, obedience, appreciation, belonging, and love as their essential expressions. Where the framework is denied and the foundation destroyed natural and moral development – growing up – is beset with difficulties.

It is in the nature of sin to rebel against and deny the natural and moral obligations of life or, to put it biblically, to transgress the law, or, again, to break covenant. The natural and moral order that lies at the heart of essential human relationships is a manifestation of the law of the Lord. It is that law, or word of the Lord, that is declared in Scripture to be the foundation for covenant, and covenant is the arrangement upon which relationship with God, and with others, is securely established and enjoyed.

Fathers are covenant figures

Covenant, in Scripture, is foundational to all relationship and relating. It is, however, this very foundation that is missing from so much of our thinking about personal relationships, certainly in the world, and increasingly in the Church. Fathers were covenantal figures; covenants were made with them and by them so that both natural and spiritual relationships were "legally" recognized, established, and secure. God said to Noah,

> "*I will establish my covenant with you, and you will enter the ark – you and your sons and your wife and your sons' wives with you.*"   (Genesis 6:18)

God entered into a covenant with Noah on behalf of all his descendants. He did the same with Abram, with Moses and the Hebrew nation, and with David, of whom he said,

> "*I will not take my love from him,*
>   *nor will I ever betray my faithfulness.*
> *I will not violate my covenant*
>   *or alter what my lips have uttered.*"   (Psalm 89:33–34)

Holiness and righteousness, so far as God is concerned, are inextricably bound up with covenant keeping – He is the God who keeps His word, His covenant word, He is therefore a holy and a righteous God. And it is upon this foundation alone, the foundation of covenant, that relationships are secure.

Covenant, then, is the framework in which those who wish to recognize or enter into a relationship, give their word and walk in the relationship together. God Himself has given His word regarding relationship with the Lord Jesus Chris,; "*I will be his Father, and he will be my Son*" (Hebrews 1:5). The divine declaration was made public on more than one occasion (Matthew 3:17 and 17:5), God giving testimony by His word to the relationship and thereby identifying the formal arrangement upon which the relationship was secure. The Holy Spirit bears witness to the covenant relationship between the Father and the Son, a covenant that lies as the eternal foundation for the life, law, and love that will eventually fill the universe with both righteousness and happiness.

In 2 Corinthians 6:16–18 Paul used the whole concept of covenant to encourage the Corinthian believers to be faithful to God. "*What agreement is there between the temple of God and idols?*" he asked – and of course there was no covenant or agreement between the two, there was nothing binding – "*for we are the temple of the living God. As God has said: 'I will live with them and walk among them, and I will be their God, and they will be*

my people,' " a clear reference to Leviticus 26:12 where God
established covenant with Israel.

> *" 'Therefore come out from them*
> *and be separate,*
> > *says the Lord.*
> *Touch no unclean thing,*
> *and I will receive you.' "* (2 Corinthians 6:17)

Then Paul continues,

> *" 'I will be a Father to you,*
> *and you will be my sons and daughters,*
> > *says the Lord Almighty.' "*
> > (2 Corinthians 6:18)

Covenant signs and symbols

A covenant is established when the word of the parties involved
is given, witnessed and sealed, sometimes with signs and sym-
bols – a rainbow, circumcision, rings, blood, bread and wine, and
more. Often the covenant, and thus the relationship, is comme-
morated in regular celebration and thanksgiving – the Passover,
birthdays, wedding anniversaries, the Lord's Supper, church
covenant days, and so on.

So fundamental is covenant to relationship that Scripture,
God's word written, is itself called the Old Covenant (Testament)
and the New Covenant. Scripture, therefore, is a covenant
document, the inscripted word, that forms the foundation for
relationship with the Father. God's Son, the Lord Jesus Christ, is
the Word incarnate in whom the word inscripted is perfectly
fulfilled. The New Covenant in which all believers have fellowship with God is established by the obedience of the incarnate
Word to the inscripted word. It is this covenant relationship
between the Father and the Son, administered by the Holy Spirit
in the gospel (the good news of the New Covenant), that
underwrites all spiritual relationship and relating. There is no
relationship with God apart from covenant.

When the essential element of covenant is removed from
relationship we are left with nothing but feelings of attraction,
fancies, and personal preferences. The giving of my word is

ndered to the gratifying of my feelings, I am bound to
nothing but self-satisfaction. Salvation on this premise would
be uncertain, marriage short-lived, family insecure, friendship
hesitant, and fellowship tentative.

It is the word of the Lord, however, that stands as an everlasting testimony to the assurance and certainty of all true
relationship, *"he will remain faithful, for he cannot disown himself"*
(2 Timothy 2:13). In Christ we stand in covenant relationship
with God. If we understand this it both informs and inspires all
other relationships – salvation is certain, marriage life-long,
family secure, friendship strong and fellowship sure. The tragedy
is that notwithstanding all the contemporary teaching and
emphasis on relationships, failure in this very area has increased
enormously: believers are uncertain and need various extra-
biblical props and excitements to "keep them going," marriages
are precarious, families insecure, friendships fragile, and fellowship fragmentary. The disregard of formal recognition, agreement, and arrangement based on the integrity and faithfulness
of one's word is a major reason for this.

Relationship to fathers recognizes principles of covenant

Covenant breaking affects the entire structure of human relationships because it rejects law, authority, obedience, and duty. In the
recognition of fathers and fathering we begin again to recognize
principles of covenant, of relationship based on the authority
of law and responsibility rooted in the integrity of one's word.
And we may, if by God's grace we continue to follow the path,
eventually come to confess that Jesus Christ is Lord, for all
temporal law and authority has its origin in the sovereign
authority given Him *by* the Father for the glory *of* the Father.
The recognition and acknowledgement of some temporal yet
legitimate covenant, such as marriage, fatherhood or family, in
natural life may lead on to a recognition later of covenant in the
larger, spiritual and eternal realm. The perception of divine order
in the natural world may be a fundamental element in the Spirit's
work of prevenient grace. Such recognition will not save us, but
may bring conviction that will lead to repentance, for

> *"the law is holy, and the commandment is holy, righteous and*
> *good. Did that which is good, then, become death to me? By no*

means! But in order that sin might be recognized as sin, it produced death in me through what was good, so that through the commandment sin might become utterly sinful." (Romans 7:12–13)

The disparagement of respect for rules, commandment, authority, and headship in favor of personal right, corporate tolerance, and behavioral choice will inevitably deride marriage, fatherhood, and family because these are repositories of lawful covenant.

A spiritual father can function only as his word is trusted, received, and recognized and a relationship established. If we doubt a father's word we will find it well nigh impossible to accept his care, counsel, and love. Many people want to receive God's "love" – have a relationship with Him – without any recognition of His word. Some go so far as claiming relationship with Him while doubting, and even rejecting, His word.

I have sought to show that relationship without covenant leads to living without responsibility, a flawed and fragile framework in which authority goes unrecognized, counsel unheeded, and love misunderstood. True fathering and mentoring in this case, though often asked for, may not be readily received.

Furthermore fathers themselves may be seriously affected by a reluctance to accept both responsibility and the mandate to administrate God's covenant word faithfully. We must locate our thinking and expectations regarding fathering and mentoring in the biblical context. Divorced from theology and doctrine they will be nothing but psychological means and methods.

Those willing to accept the designation of father must themselves submit to the covenant foundations of Scripture lest relationships are built with impressionable sons on the basis of public persona and celebrity status, on popularity and "success," on relationship unsupported by covenant and charisma unconfirmed by character.

We come back, therefore, as always, to our resting place, to our Head and Source, to God our Father, the covenant-keeping God, and to Jesus, the Mediator of a New Covenant. Fathers and mentors in spiritual union with the Father and the Son will have serious regard to covenant-keeping and will function by the integrity of their character and the faithfulness of their word. They may establish upon that foundation a covenant and a relationship with others in which their authority, care, and counsel carries both weight and worth.

Chapter 6

Fathers – Truth and Doctrine

Relationships in the empirical sense, while valuable (if right), should not, as we have been saying, be pushed to an unwarranted level. Though they are ever-present they are not all-important and we will be damaged if we elevate them to such a position.

For example, loyalty to a relationship must not take precedence over commitment to truth. The apostle Paul said to Timothy *"You ... know all about my teaching, my way of life, my purpose, faith, patience, love, endurance"* (2 Timothy 3:10). Paul clearly saw his teaching and his life as all of a piece, but put teaching first because his way of life was the outcome of what he believed. The writer to the Hebrews wrote similarly,

> *"Remember your leaders, who spoke the word of God to you.*
> *Consider the outcome of their way of life and imitate their faith."*
> (Hebrews 13:7)

It is important that we know something about those who teach us truth – general knowledge of those who address churches at large by means of common reputation, and more specific knowledge of those who pastor and teach us on a regular basis by means of personal association. But Scripture, truth, and doctrine are not subservient to relationships. As we shall see later, a teacher through whom God passes truth *is* important, but not all-important, and the teacher who claims that what he teaches is right and good because he is teaching it is placing himself and relationship with himself above the truth.

It is not uncommon for people to believe something to be true because of their admiration for the person teaching it. Some are quickly impressed by an authoritative style or by the aura of confidence created by media presentation or celebrity status. To query accepted and highly acclaimed teachers is not popular or easy, to question them (not always easy either) may be thought pompous or arrogant. Nevertheless wise leaders and teachers, celebrated or otherwise, hold themselves accountable to others and allow that accountability to be common knowledge. Teachers who stand beyond question and honest examination neglect both humility and wisdom.

Spiritual fathers know only too well that their foibles and frailties will sooner or later become clear to their "children" simply because a large part of their ministry involves personal interaction with them. Spiritual fathers, together with pastors with whom they share many qualities, are most likely to be "known" because personal association makes it difficult to preserve leadership mystique or an air of didactic infallibility.

Paul and the Corinthians

It is quite true that, so far as teaching was concerned, the apostle Paul did claim a specific and unique authority for the gospel he preached (Galatians 1:6–12). The claim, however, was not based upon it being "his" gospel in the sense that its origin was in him but on its being a divine revelation to him, a revelation plainly declared and open to reason, examination, and verification. This is why, in his gospel preaching and teaching, Paul *"reasoned . . . from the Scriptures, explaining and proving that the Christ had to suffer and rise from the dead"* (Acts 17:2–3). Furthermore he was perfectly willing for his hearers to *"examine the Scriptures every day to see if what* [he] *said was true"* (Acts 17:11), in order for the authenticity of his ministry to be established.

Paul was unhappy with the Corinthian believers because their claim to truth was rooted in their attachment to various leaders and teachers, *"I follow Paul," "I follow Apollos," "I follow Christ"* (1 Corinthians 1:12). Those who claimed to follow Christ were no better than the others because they were using His name in their own interests and for sectarian ends. To be sure, only Jesus can say, "I am the truth," hence truly knowing Him is to know the One who is the sum and substance of all truth. This cannot be said of any other relationship. It does not mean, however, that by knowing Him I have some form of immediate understanding of all truth – though some foolish people come close to

claiming this. My attachment and relationship to Christ does
stand above all other relationships. It is unique. Yet even this
relationship, one that we might call a saving relationship, stands
essentially related to truth, for Jesus Himself said,

> *"If you love me, you will obey what I command . . . Whoever has*
> *my commands and obeys them, he is the one who loves me . . .*
> *If anyone loves me he will obey my teaching."*
>
> (John 14:15, 21, 23)[1]

Paul's concern over the Corinthian attitude to truth and doctrine is a concern shared by all spiritual fathers, namely that
doctrine must not be used to create sectarian division,[2] but be
properly held in order to identify us as Christian believers and
establish our behavior as children of God. The Corinthians were
turning Christ's ministers and the profound truths and doctrines
of the gospel entrusted to them into frivolous instruments of
party strife. True spiritual fathers will not use doctrine for their
own ends in this way, either to create a faction or establish a
reputation. And they will, like Paul, deplore such a use of truth in
those they mentor with words similar to Paul's:

> *"Brothers, I could not address you as spiritual but as worldly –*
> *mere infants in Christ."*   (1 Corinthians 3:1)

Doctrine on the defensive

We live at a time when truth, doctrine and theology are too often
spoken of negatively, as instruments of division and discord. The
current trend is running contrary to theological definition and
precision. To lay claim to doctrinal assurance is to be dogmatic
and intolerant, even bigoted. Bob Mumford, renowned Bible
teacher, said at a conference recently, "People are joining
churches today for reasons other than truth, without any thought
of what that church holds or teaches."[3] It was a comment that
would be echoed by many spiritual fathers. It is also true that
many churches talk now about principles rather than truth and
values rather than doctrine, so that it is not always easy to
discover what a church and its leaders actually hold as a body of
"sound doctrine" (2 Timothy 4:3; Titus 1:9; 2:1).

While doctrine, however, has been receiving such bad press,

relationships have been elevated to a position of prominence. The inference is not that difficult to draw: truth and doctrine are not crucial and must defer to relationships, which are crucial. So, for example, my relationship *to* Christ and my experience *of* Christ are more important than what I believe *about* Christ. *"Who is my neighbor?"* takes precedence over Christ's question *"Who do you say I am?"* (Luke 10:29; Matthew 16:15); the quest for unity bypasses the virgin birth and the bodily resurrection of Christ;[4] and multi-faith dialogue supersedes doctrinal focus, prophetic declaration, and gospel action. Relationships therefore are deemed more important than truth because relationships call for tolerance while truth calls for decision.

The answer to all this does not lie in a return to that aggressive fundamental literalism that uses word and text to win arguments at all costs, to crush opposition and close down enquiry. It lies rather in a careful bringing of ourselves before Scripture as God's word written, in preparing ourselves to sit beneath it in humility and be judged by it in meekness, and so, by devotion to it and study of it, come to a conviction of mind and heart that transforms our living and makes us able ministers of the New Testament. It is in this way that truth and doctrine takes hold of us, informs, quickens, and illuminates our minds, sheds light on difficult questions and troublesome circumstances, lifts our heads and shows us the way forward – *"a lamp to my feet and a light for my path"* (Psalm 119:105).

Doctrine, counsel and care

Fathers know the power of Scripture to throw light upon our confusion when other counsel leaves us in gloom. They know it because, in their own personal experience, God's word, applied by His Spirit to difficult situations and problems, has brought them clarity and release. A wise mentor will take his follower to Scripture, opening it up and demonstrating its relevance to contemporary life and thought. He knows that an attachment to himself, no matter how loving, will be no substitute for his disciple appreciating and proving the sufficiency of Scripture for himself. And it isn't simply exhortation or devotional truth that is needed, or a mantra type approach to "the promises." Our believing and assurance must be rooted in the great themes and doctrines of the faith. The tendency, if we are not submitted to

Scripture in this way, is to become sentimental on the one hand, or managerial on the other. By sentimental I mean taken up with the pursuit of personal holiness on the basis of self-effort, something the apostle Paul sought to avoid in his epistles by setting out doctrine before behavior, making it the ground from which true godliness grows. By managerial I mean that form of Christianity that makes the kingdom of God and the church of Christ a business to be promoted along the lines of high-powered management, advertising and entertainment techniques, with celebrities, programs, artists, and a three ring circus.

Both sentimental and managerial models of leadership and church are seriously inadequate. The one is obsessed with a man-centered piety, the other with a man-centered personality. When we submit with love and meekness to Scripture and allow God's revelation to commend itself to us by the Holy Spirit, we assume our proper place in relation to His gracious and glorious sovereignty – *"that you may be filled to the measure of all the fullness of God"* (Ephesians 3:19).

Personal reflection

The wonder of Scripture and the majestic doctrines of salvation revealed there are a constant source of light, instruction, assurance, and delight to my mind and heart. I am inspired and motivated in those moments when Scripture glows with light and my appreciation of God's grace and glory is excited and deepened. I am fascinated by the way doctrine interrelates and forms a coherent pattern that testifies to the mind of God the Holy Spirit in His word written. To perceive something, no matter how small, of His will and purpose for humankind, creation, and the ages to come generates faith for daily assurance and understanding for a sound mind. The will of God revealed in His word is His pleasure and joy – and our strength (Nehemiah 8:10).

My love and appetite for Scripture and doctrine was awakened and nourished by a number of factors: by Don Cox, the spiritual father, elder, and teacher in my home church; by the preaching and teaching that I heard in Pentecostal conventions as a child and in my youth; by my time at the Assemblies of God Bible School at Kenley in Surrey, England;[5] by a passion for reading, and an ongoing love affair with church history.

Those Pentecostal conventions, usually Easter, Whitsun, and

bank holidays, were wonderful times. They breathed the air of Pentecostal revival. Two preachers in the afternoon and two in the evening on the Saturday, and the same again on the Monday. Believers were stirred by outstanding ministry, almost entirely expositional, from men filled with the Holy Spirit and fire – Eric Dando, Clyde Young, John and Howard Carter, Eddie Taylor, David Powell, James Forsyth, W.T.H. Richards, Jim McConnell, Ian MacPherson, Donald Gee, Robert Fairnie, Dennis Clark, John Phillips, Keith Monument, Alex Tee.[6] What preachers and teachers! And many of them fathers to the leaders and churches of the classic Pentecostal movements – and beyond. My memories as a child include wondering whenever the meetings would end and sandwiches in the intervals, but also, as I grew older, a realization that there was something very special about preaching where those who could not get in to hear it sat or stood outside looking and listening through the windows.

On many occasions I was stirred. As a student, years later, when I heard John Phillips preach on Ephesians 1 and 2 at a great conference I thought my heart would burst. I recall with awe how hundreds of people stood and cheered and clapped and worshiped at the sheer glory of the word of the Lord. I knew beyond everything else in my life that I wanted to preach and teach that word.

So, in the ministry and counsel that I bring to leaders and churches from time to time there is always reference to Scripture, to doctrine, and to theology. I am assured that it is not really possible to love God without loving the truth about Him, for how could we know who He is and what He is like without the revelation He has given of Himself in His word?

In helping and encouraging leaders I invariably find myself, after a while, rehearsing some great doctrine or line of truth and seeking to show that as we think it through there can be a release of divine light and life into our lives and the circumstances surrounding us. There is in the gospel of God, in its many facets and features, a medicine for our hearts. I recognize that not all spiritual fathers turn to Scripture and doctrine so readily and that those who do so are probably ministry gift teachers, but I am equally certain that, no matter what gift we may be, Scripture, truth, and doctrine lie central to our function.

When I am teaching, the look of dawning light and comprehension on a listener's face brings very great satisfaction to my heart (there is another look that says "I am completely in the dark," which I also see from time to time). We know that *"Understanding is a fountain of life to those who have it"* (Proverbs 16:22), that Christ Himself is revealed *"in all the Scriptures"* (Luke 24:27), and that the Holy Spirit is released through the word ministered.

Because of such convictions I pray for a renewal and a recovery of expository preaching and teaching; not a return to some former "golden age" of ministry but for God's people now, and in the future, to know the profound spiritual satisfaction, assurance, and fulfillment that comes from the breaking open of "the living bread."

In one of his International Letters on trends that have weakened churches in recent years, Barney Coombs, who heads up the Salt and Light network and pastors a church in Vancouver, refers to "Topical populist-style preaching replacing expositional teaching, the band with its drums at the centre replacing the pulpit, and subjective choruses replacing many Scriptural songs and hymns." In the midst of a world-wide outpouring of the Holy Spirit that lasted throughout the twentieth century and into the twenty-first, with the massive church increase and expansion that has accompanied it, we must continue to receive and hear mature and godly fathers encouraging us to biblical and doctrinal literacy so that experience of God, being wedded to knowledge of God, may create in us the consciousness of life eternal accompanied by demonstrations of the kingdom of God.

In his latest book Michael Green is quite specific, "The level of teaching in many churches is deplorable, and doesn't give anyone any apologetics. Of course there are honorable exceptions, but too few sermons grasp issues of truth."[7] Barney Coombs, again, makes a similar point: "With the level of biblical illiteracy we see among evangelicals today – particularly in the new churches – such an exhortation as 2 Tim 4:1–3 is certainly relevant to our generation. By and large there is very little expository teaching taking place on a typical Sunday in our churches."[8]

Evangelicals and Charismatics, given the decline in doctrinal understanding among believers, face, among a number of problems connected with that decline, one that is particularly serious. It is this. Multi-faith *action*, permissible I believe, on, for example, pro-life issues, or pornography, or pedophilia, drug addiction or terrorism, is liable now to stray on into multi-faith *worship*. The increasing lack of coherent biblical and doctrinal understanding and definition leaves "believers" exposed to the "fascination" and call of the multi-faith world, a world that denies the deity and unique Saviorhood of the Lord Jesus Christ. Joel Edwards, General Director of the Evangelical Alliance in the UK, discussing the advantages of multi-faith action (sometimes called co-belligerence), is right when he goes on to say, "I would categorically not share in an expression of worship with other faiths. Once you move into a worship context, you are then in an impossible position to protect or advocate the unique claims of Jesus. They become just one among many, and that is not the truth."[9]

Alarm at the lack of Bible reading and understanding

I must take some pains to explain what is meant by exposition of Scripture. It isn't that easy. Because this book is not a book on preaching and teaching the explanation will need to be brief but I would like to attempt it all the same, and for this reason at least: all the recent and contemporary spiritual fathers I know include the local church's need for exposition of Scripture among their major concerns. There is alarm at the lack of both Bible reading and biblical understanding among believers. To be sure, there is no lack of speakers. Evangelical opinion and charismatic ideas are readily available, events great and small are served by many able communicators handling topics and subjects which they support by reference to Scripture. However, the actual opening up of Scripture itself, looking at passages, examining and explaining text and context, whether account, narrative, or argument (particularly argument), showing and expounding the writer's meaning – in short, exposition – is rare. Why is this so? If Scripture is, in truth, the word of God written should it not be our central act of worship to come before it and hear it expounded by those given by Jesus to do that very thing? And should not those persons be set aside to seek God for both guidance on what part of His word should be expounded, and for nothing less than the anointing of the Holy Spirit to enable them to study and preach it with understanding, faith, clarity, and authority? What could possibly be more important? As John Piper says,

"The Word of God that saves and sanctifies, from generation to generation, is preserved in a book. And therefore at the heart of every pastor's work is bookwork. Call it reading, meditation, reflection, cogitation, study, exegesis, or whatever you will – a large and central part of our work is to wrestle God's meaning from a book, and then proclaim it in the power of the Holy Spirit."[10]

The sheer excitement and sense of anticipation stirred by the knowledge that we are to hear nothing less than the word of the one true and living God expounded and declared by one of His servants specifically called and sent by Him must surely be recovered. If it is not we shall be left at the last with nothing but the debris and driftwood of natural skill and entertainment dressed in the tattered rags of neo-evangelical "orthodoxy" frantically seeking to engage with a post-modern culture of social-speak and "spiritual" correctness. Sophistication will have come to church and the voice of the fathers will cry in the wilderness.

The counseling revolution

Spiritual fathers and mentors are not, first and foremost, counselors. They are servants of God's word, of the gospel of God. That word, as we are reminding ourselves, is both "His rod and His staff," our guide and our comfort. Fathers know this. They will encourage us to come before it, take it to our minds and hearts, sit in submission beneath it and receive its instruction and assurance. From there they will exhort us to labor faithfully in the study of it as a *"workman who does not need to be ashamed and who correctly handles the word of truth"* (2 Timothy 2:15).

The rise and popularity of counseling[11] is a phenomenon of the late twentieth and early twenty-first century. I unhesitatingly suggest that the flood tide of counseling in churches has taken place alongside an ebb tide of understanding regarding the nature and need of the pastor and teacher gift-ministry, of regular exposition of Scripture, and clear personal application of truth. A high percentage of the problems being dealt with by counselors are related directly or indirectly to the sins and excesses of "western" society and culture. They are a result of not understanding ourselves spiritually, socially, and physically. This lack of understanding, the outcome of sin as a result of transgressing the law of the Lord, is addressed in the gospel. The more we understand the gospel – the revelation of God, His being and His kingdom; man and his condition; Christ and His nature, cross, and resurrection; God the Holy Spirit at work in the world; the life and position of the Christian believer; and the nature and work of local churches – the more we will understand ourselves and our circumstances. The almost obsessive need felt by many Christians for personal counseling would be dramatically reduced by a return to anointed, regular, lucid exposition of Scripture accompanied by clear application and normal pastoral follow-up where necessary. This is to make no criticism of Christian friendship and fellowship where normal conversation on all kinds of spiritual, doctrinal, and personal matters may take place as part of the natural intercourse of life. That is a necessary part of a healthy Christian life and a lively local church.

Handling problems doctrinally

When a problem arises and crowds in upon a church leader or team, it can become overwhelming. Our peace is disturbed and we become troubled in mind and heart; we grow weary examining the situation from every angle, and we struggle to see a way of handling it. Sometimes the issue disturbs our sleep and we lie awake – what are we to do? How are we to resolve it? Why has it happened?

Answers rarely come by constantly "worrying" a problem. Analysis – taking it to pieces, poring over it, looking at it – tends to magnify an issue until the mind is tired. Fathers help us to turn aside and look at something larger and greater. The problems and troubles of church and ministry will find their true proportion in the greater scheme of God's will and revelation as we learn to reflect on doctrine. To contemplate some great truth, some aspect of God's sovereign love in His plan of salvation, is solace for a sore heart and a place of rest for a troubled mind. To consider a problem on the grounds of "such a great salvation" will keep us in balance (Hebrews 2:3).

Spiritual fathers tend to face such difficulties with a measure of calm. One reason for this is a mind settled and rooted deep in the soil of God's word. Composure of spirit rests easy in the great doctrines of Scripture and their cohesive nature. They provide a perspective on life, a world view that is not easily distracted by trouble or disturbed by distress. This kind of underlying settled-ness, however, does not mean entire absence of restless nights. We may still have them, though such waves on the surface do not necessarily indicate disturbance in the deep. I've tossed my way through a troubled night on too many occasions. I usually end up wandering, sleepy eyed, into my study and musing among my books, lighting more often than not upon Oswald Chambers, Martyn Lloyd-Jones, P.T. Forsyth or Ephesians 1, 2, and 3!

It is often at times like this that spiritual fathers come along-side to guide leaders and teams with care, insight, and wisdom through a maze of arguments and sometimes extreme opinions. While not always theologians in the strict sense of the word they may articulate theology with easy logic, reason, and persuasion, and will, often, step unerringly through an argument and help us to reason our way through to a biblical understanding and a godly position. A father will help us to think: "Perhaps," he will say, "you are in danger of being swayed by a clever presentation, or a winning personality, or a fascinating theory. Stop for a moment, think, reflect." He will show us other passages, ask us other questions, and, extremely importantly, help us to follow through the implications of what we are considering. "Can you see," he may say, "where this line of thought is leading? Look at the moral implications, look at the practical outcome, see where it is taking you." The implications may be dangerous, or they may be glorious, opening for us fresh perspectives that both stimulate our understanding and transform our living. Theo-logians will often lift us into the wonder of truth, fathers will help us to see how that truth applies to our life or sheds light on a problem.

Those men who have been my fathers have all led me to Scripture and to Christ, always to both in union and without contradiction. I realized early on that I could not have the incarnate Word without believing the written word in which He was set before me by the Holy Spirit. There has always been a tendency to polarize around "I am a person of the word," or "I am a person of the Spirit," or even "I am a simple follower of Christ, doctrine confuses me and the Holy Spirit is odd." These and similar expressions drive a wedge between God's word written and God's Word incarnate, a dichotomy not sanctioned by Scripture or by Christ.

"Come now, let us reason together" (Isaiah 1:18)

Fathers are often good, but not always great preachers. However, a true spiritual father, if not himself a great preacher or teacher, will have a high view of Scripture and the study of it. And the ability to minister Scripture into a life is not necessarily synonymous with a powerful platform ministry. Fathers know that God has revealed Himself in Scripture and in Christ and that out of that divine and mysterious union proceeds a revelation which is life eternal.

Fatherly concern for our intellectual and rational development, therefore, has its origin in God Himself, who says, *"Come now, let us reason together."* Here is an invitation to sit together, to talk things through, to relate at the level of the mind and engage one another's thought processes. Can it really be true that God Himself wants to do this with us? Is it possible that my mind can engage in any way with the mind of God, for the drop to reason with the ocean? We can indeed say that this is possible because He Himself calls us to do it. The wonder is that in bringing Him my mind, rather than losing it by some absorption in His vastness, I find it uniquely touched and released to think thoughts *"too wonderful for me"* (Psalm 139:6), to an illumination that spreads its light through every part and brings a knowing that is exquisite in its ability to satisfy. God knows that He is like this for us – that is why He calls us to sit and think with Him. It was like this in the beginning with Adam. Since Adam turned away to walk in darkness, God has been working out His unchanging desire, at infinite cost through Christ His Son, to bring us back to walk with Him again. It is His will to so think and talk with us that the light and glory of truth will illuminate our darkened minds again and we begin, slowly, to know what He always intended we should know, the true, life-giving, holy and abundant nature of His character and delight – "This is what I am really like."

There is little to compare with the anguish in the heart of a lover when the love is misunderstood and rejected by its sole object. *"God so loved the world,"* and the pleasure of His heart is fulfilled in His commending that love toward us in His Son – and having us receive it. True spiritual fathers reflect the desire and delight of our Father in heaven and so they also often say, "Let's sit down and think this through together . . ."

Notes

1. Jesus was teaching that those who truly love Him will, because they love Him, find in themselves a willing delight to obey Him. He was not saying that the essence of love for Himself lies in obedience to His teaching but that a heart of love for Him will in its very nature love His teaching and obey His commands. It might seem to be a fine distinction but the fault reveals itself if we misunderstand the issue to the extent that we make adherence to a school of doctrine or code of conduct the defining mark of love for Christ.

2. This is not to say that truth and doctrine does not create division, it does. Simply holding it probably creates more division than anything else. Holding it, however, is quite different to using it to bring about division.

3. A Groundlevel Leaders' conference in Lincoln in June 2002.

4. Please don't imagine that I am overstating the case for the purpose of effect. I am not. I have been challenged by "evangelicals" to hold both the virgin birth and the bodily resurrection of our Lord Jesus Christ loosely in the cause of unity.

5. A school committed to the life and ministry of the Spirit and the study and preaching of the Word, where my life was enriched, my passion fuelled, and my mind stirred to think.

6. I realize quite well that these names may mean little to those familiar only with the mainstream evangelical world of the mid and later twentieth century. Most of these men, and many others, were fathers and sons of the classic Pentecostal revival, pioneers of a movement of the Holy Spirit that would, by the close of the twentieth century, circle the earth. They were apostles, prophets, evangelists, teachers and pastors who would have stood easily among the evangelical preachers and leaders of the time were it not for their holding to a doctrine and experience of the Spirit that, in their day, largely excluded them. That is history now, and time has happily moved on – but I take great pleasure in mentioning and honoring their names. They were my fathers.

7. *But Don't all Religions Lead to God?* (Sovereign World/IVP, 2002).

8. Barney Coombs, *Apostles Today* (Sovereign World, 1996), p. 32.

9. From *Idea* (magazine of the UK Evangelical Alliance) September 2002, in an article entitled "Choosing the Right Words."

10. *The Legacy of Sovereign Joy* (IVP, 2000). John Piper's book, especially the section on Sacred Study from which this quote is taken, is very good. Its contribution to the Word and Spirit debate, against the background of well-researched history, is first class.

11. By this I mean formal or semi-formal one-to-one sessions in which various formula are employed that concentrate upon an individual's conscious or sub-conscious feelings, fears, inhibitions, and background. This is often connected, in "Christian" counseling, with reference to unnatural, abnormal or demonic influences in the person's past. Group counseling sessions may also run along these or similar lines.

   A major emphasis in counseling therefore shifts the focus from God the Father and the Lord Jesus Christ to me and all things to do with me. A true biblical anthropology locates the meaning and object of my life in God, not in myself, in my heavenly Father, not in my personal ego, in relationship to Him, not in realization of me. A true exposition of the gospel of God redeems my life, renews my mind, and transforms my living by direct reference to what God has done for me in His Son. I need to hear this gospel preached in all its glorious dimensions, *"to grasp how wide and long and high and deep is the love of Christ, and to know this love that surpasses knowledge . . . "* (Ephesians 3:18–19). Regular exposure to this highest of all truth, with application of it to my life, will be the best of all medicines, the sweetest of all sounds, the answer to all fears.

Chapter 7

Fathers – and the Holy Spirit

Is it merely noteworthy that baptism in the Spirit is described by Jesus as *"the gift my Father promised"* (Acts 1:4)? Surely not. In the beginning God breathed His life into Adam and walked in love with him, Father and son in fellowship. God, the one true and eternal Spirit, breathed His spirit, the very "breath of life," into Adam (*"the Spirit gives birth to spirit,"* John 3:6) and Adam became a living being (Genesis 2:7). He lived and walked in His Father's spirit, ate from the Tree of Life, and by the obedience of faith which expresses itself by love (Galatians 5:6), grew in the knowledge of his Father, which is eternal life.

The Father and Adam in the beginning

There are no words we can use to describe adequately the loss brought about by Adam's sin. The fall itself has deprived us of a full understanding of the life enjoyed in the Spirit by the Father and Adam.[1] Nevertheless, God graciously reveals the loss to us through His word by the same Spirit; we call it conviction of sin and even a little of it is appalling. The only appropriate response to this conviction is confession, repentance toward God, and faith in Christ, all of which, under such conviction, we may long to carry out only to discover the terrible truth that we are entirely unable to do so. It is the love and mercy of God, who, in the person of His Son, the Lord Jesus Christ, takes upon Himself our sin, shows us its nature in the cross and by that same cross pays for it, convicts us of our ungodly and lost condition, and meets us in the extremity of that condition with the wondrous gifts of repentance and faith. We come before Him with such priceless treasures only to discover again that they are fruits of a new life that has already begun in us through God's sovereign grace. We have been born of the Spirit. And we have been born *of* the Spirit in order that we might be baptized *in* the Spirit and filled *with* the Spirit. This is what Jesus was referring to when He spoke of His Father's promise,

> *"Do not leave Jerusalem, but wait for the gift my Father promised, which you have heard me speak about. For John baptized with water, but in a few days you will be baptized in the Holy Spirit."*
> (Acts 1:4–5)

Peter, preaching with anointed courage on the Day of Pentecost, instructed those under conviction to repent, be baptized, and then receive their heavenly Father's awesome blessing, the wondrous, praising, worshiping, working, witnessing, signing, and sealing gift of the Holy Spirit.

Born *of* the Spirit to be baptized *in* the Spirit

Precious things follow upon our being born again: we begin to see the kingdom of God; we turn from our sins to believe on the Lord Jesus Christ; we are baptized in His name; we receive the gift of the Holy Spirit. Our eyes, therefore, are opened to God's kingdom, the realm and order in which God created us to live, and through repentance and faith in the Lord Jesus Christ we are immersed in, and filled with, the Holy Spirit so that we can seek and serve that kingdom. God's purpose for His children has not changed. We are called to walk in His life or spirit, come to know His being and nature, and gladly serve the interests of His kingdom.

The connection between the Father and baptism in the Spirit is blessedly clear – it is His gift of authentication, authority, and power for His redeemed children. Jesus said:

> *"If you then, though you are evil, know how to give good gifts to your children, how much more will your Father in heaven give the Holy Spirit to those who ask him!"* (Luke 11:13)

Our restoration to God's plan and purpose has been accomplished through the life, death, resurrection, and ascension of

His Son, the Lord Jesus Christ. Because of our union with Him we may, now, be baptized in, and filled with, the Holy Spirit, the Father's gift.

The seal of the Spirit authenticates the sons of God

So far as Jesus the Son is concerned the descent of the Holy Spirit upon Him *"in bodily form like a dove"* was accompanied by His Father's voice from heaven, *"You are my Son, whom I love; with you I am well pleased"* (Luke 3:22). Jesus knew, at the commencement of His ministry, the comfort and encouragement of His Father's affirmation. Before He had preached a word or worked a miracle His Father identified and owned Him publicly as His Son, declared His love for Him and proclaimed His pleasure in Him. There is little to compare with the comfort and assurance felt by children when they are identified, owned, and publicly blessed by their fathers. Little wonder that Jesus spoke afterwards of the gift of the Holy Spirit as the promise of the Father, a Counselor sent in His, Jesus', name (John 14:26). Paul later encouraged the Ephesian Christians with the same truth. He said:

> *"Having believed, you were marked in him with a seal, the promised Holy Spirit."*   (Ephesians 1:13)

Identity and authority walk hand in hand. Baptism in the Spirit is at once the Father's seal of identity and ownership on us as His children, and the fullness of divine authority and power in us as His witnesses. By the Spirit we are identified and affirmed as sons, we know who we are; and by the same Spirit we are authorized and energized as servants, we know what we must do:

> *"you will receive power when the Holy Spirit comes on you; and you will be my witnesses in Jerusalem, and in all Judea and Samaria, and to the ends of the earth."*   (Acts 1:8)

Witness and worship by the Spirit

It is not too much to say that fatherhood and fathering is essentially connected with identifying children, with owning, affirming, and forming them as sons and daughters and equipping them to speak the truth as servants and witnesses. Christian witness may be defined, very simply, as living and speaking the truth about our Father through His Son by the Spirit. Christian worship may be defined as acknowledging and confessing the Father through the Son by the same Spirit. Some of the great hymns are excellent examples of acknowledging and confessing God as our Father, for example:

> "Holy, Holy, Holy, Lord God Almighty,
> All Thy works shall praise Thy name,
>   in earth and sky and sea,
> Holy, holy, holy, merciful and mighty,
> God in three persons, blessed trinity."[2]

We will, therefore, by the Spirit and through the Son (in His name), bear witness to, and give worship to, the Father. And because the Spirit is the Spirit of truth our witness to the Father will be a witness to the truth about Him, it will be a theological witness. The same must be said about worship. When the Father's children bring Him worship it will be *"in spirit and in truth"* (John 4:24), that is, it will be both devotional and doctrinal. This is what we mean when we say that theology, the truth about God, stands at the heart of our witness and our worship.

A chief characteristic of spiritual fathering

I would like to carry the connection between the Father and the Spirit a little further. It is by the Spirit that the Father makes Himself known. In the events of the Old Testament, for instance, God's revelation of Himself is always a work of the Holy Spirit. It is a communication of truth about His being and nature that comes to its full New Testament expression through the ministry of the Lord Jesus Christ, and, again, by the direct agency of the Holy Spirit. The essential ministry of the Holy Spirit in the Son's witness to the Father is testimony to the need for every child of God to receive a fullness of the Spirit's person and power in order to witness to the Father and the Son. Just as the Spirit is central to all divine testimony – to the Father's testimony to the Son and the Son's testimony to the Father – so He is central to all spiritual fatherhood and sonship.

A capacity for knowing the Spirit and encouraging sons to live and walk in His presence and power is a chief characteristic of spiritual fathering. It is why Paul, on meeting the disciples in Ephesus (Acts 19:1–7), immediately inquired of them, *"Did you receive the Holy Spirit when* [or after] *you believed?"* He was concerned that they were, as he wrote to the Ephesians later, *"marked in him with a seal, the promised Holy Spirit"* (Ephesians 1:13).

The Christian believer's life is life in the Spirit, and central to that life is the promise of the Father, the gift of the Spirit. A true spiritual father will plead passionately for all God's children to receive the Father's promised gift. He knows there is no substitute for baptism in the Spirit.

For fathering and mentoring to reach beyond natural advice, counseling, and persuasion into spiritual authentication of life and ministry, there will have to be a fullness of the Spirit. How well the apostle Paul knew this. He wrote,

> *"When I came to you, brothers, I did not come with eloquence or superior wisdom as I proclaimed to you the testimony about God. For I resolved to know nothing while I was with you except Jesus Christ and him crucified. I came to you in weakness and fear, and with much trembling. My message and my preaching were not with wise and persuasive words, but with a demonstration of the Spirit's power, so that your faith might not rest on men's wisdom, but on God's power."*   (1 Corinthians 2:1–5)

In the field of leadership and contemporary church growth there is an almost stifling excess of "how to do it" literature, of strategy, goal-thinking, market-research-oriented technique and models. It is an emphasis difficult to find in the New Testament.[3] Of course there is guidance and instruction on the mission and ministry of the people of God in the world, in both Old Testament biography and narrative and New Testament precept and principle (especially in the Acts and the pastoral epistles), but the great note, the dominating note, is not management, method, and formula, but calling, character, and the wondrous ministry of the Spirit.

Crucial questions for the Galatians – and for us

We so urgently need those fathers and mentors who know the Holy Spirit's presence and power, who *"keep in step with the Spirit"*

(Galatians 5:25), and minister by His leading and discernment. Paul fathered like this and it led to his upbraiding the Galatians directly and with passion:

> *"Are you so foolish? After beginning with the Spirit, are you now trying to attain your goal by human effort?"*   (Galatians 3:3)

It was a crucial question for them at the time, and it is a crucial question for us now. For them the question involved the doctrinal foundations of the gospel and the future of the Christian Church. For us the question calls for a radical assessment of what we believe spiritual growth and progress to be, for both individuals and churches. Spiritual fathers will insist on this kind of question because they know that it lies at the very heart of Christian authenticity. They know that if our birth, growth and development is not by the Spirit, it is not Christian at all. So deeply did Paul feel this that he questioned the Galatians in the most remarkable terms, asking, *"Who has bewitched you?"* Strong fathering indeed. Yet such honest judgment and enquiry is all part of a father's concern, which may be expressed in queries such as, "Are you believing for the anointing of the Spirit?"; "Are you seeking Him and walking with Him at the moment?"; "Have you been affected by the Holy Spirit's presence in your private life in recent days, in your study, your praying, your preaching?" Put in this way such inquiries sound rather like a formal process of interrogation, in fact they are more likely to be part of spontaneous conversations integral to a positive ongoing relationship. Spiritual fathers and mentors form life by relationship rather than force action by formula.

The Holy Spirit, and ministry of God's word

An effective ministry of God's word releases the presence and power of the Holy Spirit. In fact the word of God and the Spirit of God are of one essence: His Spirit is His breath, His life, and that life comes forth by His word. God speaks and His Spirit moves. This is why the gospel is described as *"the word of life"* (Philippians 2:16, my emphasis).

Ministry of that word "flows" in the Spirit. When a leader who is finding ministry[4] difficult and preaching dry seeks a father's encouragement, the kindly answer will almost certainly be along the lines of, "Put down your books, leave the Internet alone, stop trying all kinds of ideas, and come to the Lord Jesus Christ Himself. Seek Him, get close to Him, and 'drink' of Him. Tell Him that this is what you want to do." Christ, the anointed One, is the source of the life flow of the Spirit from within us. Jesus cried,

> *" 'If anyone is thirsty, let him **come to me and drink**. Whoever believes in me, as the Scripture has said, streams of living water will flow from within him.' By this he meant the Spirit, whom those who believed in him were later to receive. Up to that time the Spirit had not been given, since Jesus had not yet been glorified."*
> (John 7:37–39, my emphasis)

The remedy for a dry life and a heavy ministry, therefore, is internal rather than external. It is in our relationship to the Spirit through communion with the Lord Jesus Christ. The "flow" and unction in ministry for which we all long has nothing to do with a low voice cooing over soft music, it is the essential life of the Spirit of God within us released by that Spirit through ministry of His word. Loving spiritual fathers and mentors know this and will inquire after the quality of our attachment and devotion to Christ and encourage us on (or back) into personal fellowship with Him.

Christ is the Baptizer in the Spirit – *"I baptize you with water for repentance,"* said John Baptist. *"But after me will come one who is more powerful than I, whose sandals I am not fit to carry. He will baptize you with the Holy Spirit and with fire"* (Matthew 3:11). Fathers will indicate this as the way forward, "Drink of Christ. Be filled with the Spirit. Pray with the Spirit. Let your inner man be strengthened in the Spirit." This is the source of the divine flow that inspires study, ministry, and delivery, the life of the Spirit within.

Spirit, breath, word and life

There is no need to be confused between the Spirit and the word. The breath of God that is His life is the same breath that speaks His word: His word is His breath. That is why the life of God is in the word of God because the word of God is the breath of God.

"The words I have spoken to you," said Jesus, *"are spirit and they are life"* (John 6:63). When we preach God's word, therefore, we *"hold out the word of life"* (Philippians 2:16). Why is it the word of life? Because it is the spirit, the breath, the life of God. This is what the apostle Paul intended Timothy, his son in the faith, to understand by the words, *"All Scripture is God-breathed ..."* (2 Timothy 3:16).

It is perfectly proper, therefore, to distinguish between word and Spirit but quite wrong to separate word and Spirit, for they are of the same essence. When we preach and teach the word there is a release of the Spirit. He comes forth *in* the word as witness *to* the word; He is both communicator and interpreter. If this excites the comment, "Then I don't need to give attention to exposition or delivery, the Spirit will do it all," the wise father and mentor will reply, "No, that is not the case. Clarity of communication and exposition of truth is all part of Spirit-anointed preparation and presentation." The Spirit will witness *to* the preacher as he opens the word in his study before He witnesses *through* the preacher as he declares the word to the people.

My plea for a recovery of regular exposition of Scripture is not simply a father's cry for a past long gone. Not at all. It is a call to awaken faith for that illuminating preaching of the gospel of God *"by the Holy Spirit sent from heaven"* (1 Peter 1:12), that feeds the mind, quickens the heart, stirs the soul, deepens the life, and nourishes the Spirit. In short, as Peter said, a breath of fresh air *"sent from heaven,"* that blows through meetings overloaded with songs, heavy with problem-orientated "ministry," and tense with super-spiritual hype. Heavenly breezes will disperse so much of this as they come blowing free from the word, fragrant with grace and the truth that makes us free. No, I'm not asking for a weekly long-winded verbal assault on the people of God, but the breaking of heavenly fresh-baked bread, bread that *"comes from the mouth of God"* (Matthew 4:4), the very word of life by which we live! God's people languish for lack of it, will sooner or later be sick of substitutes for it, and will weep for joy at its goodness when they get taste of it – for the Lord is good.

Sons, to the word of His grace and the free Spirit of the Lord. To change the metaphor, draw water with joy from the wells of salvation and refresh the body of Christ.

My baptism in the Spirit

The Pentecostal Mission on Millbrook Road in Southampton experienced a remarkable outpouring of the Holy Spirit in the years 1951–52. Central to this outpouring was the apostolic ministry of James Forsyth of Belfast. He originally came to the church for a week's teaching but so powerful was the effect of his ministry that he eventually stayed for seven. The whole church, including my mother and father, was caught up in this move of the Spirit, which initially lasted many months and went on to affect the life and work of the church (and surrounding churches) for many years.

On James Forsyth's visit to the church during Easter 1955[5] a meeting was arranged on the Sunday afternoon for the young people to be baptized in the Holy Spirit. With two friends, David Irish (later to become, with his wife Margaret, a remarkable church planter in Papua/New Guinea) and Mike Rothery, I went to the little room at the rear of the building with eight others. I was thirteen at the time. There were no "instructions," the doctrine of baptism in the Holy Spirit was so prevalent among us.[6] The whole church was filled with the evidence of it. We were all kneeling as James Forsyth and James Connelly laid hands on us and began to pray for us. The Holy Spirit simply filled the room and everyone in it. Every young person was baptized in the Spirit, speaking in tongues, and praising God with fluency and joy. It seemed as if but five minutes had passed when we walked unsteadily, glowing and praising, from that room to where many of the older people were waiting and praying for us in the minor hall. But we had been there over an hour, filling the room with heavenly praises while those outside sang and shouted for joy. I never doubted my salvation from that afternoon (the evening "gospel meeting" was a continuation of the outpouring) and have grieved whenever the heavenly fountain opened up in me that day has ceased to flow through sin or neglect. Jesus has always been the answer, His precious blood to cleanse us and His living Spirit to fill us. No wonder we sang,

> "Now none but Christ can satisfy,
> None other name for me,
> There's love, and life, and lasting joy,
> Lord Jesus, found in *Thee*."[7]

What do we do now?

So far as the ministry of the Spirit is concerned at the present time, it is necessary for spiritual fathers to keep their nerve, as Paul did during the Galatian crisis. During the years 1995–99 there was a great deal of prophesying, phenomena, manifestation, and spectacle. The period has left, with much assessment, some recrimination, and a fair amount of criticism, both disappointment and disillusion in its wake. At the same time, of course, there are those who quite rightly point to "the refreshing" as a source of great spiritual blessing. Others have simply gone quiet. In the aftermath of this period it is important for spiritual fathers to retain their balance and be heard to say that in spite of excess and self-indulgence the truth is still, *"'Not by might nor by power, but by my Spirit,' says the Lord Almighty"* (Zechariah 4:6).

Fathers know that, for churches to recover ground lost through dissipation, it is quite useless to retreat in reaction into some kind of compromise, into a more user-friendly mode that seeks to refashion or even redefine "church" in a more "acceptable" shape or style. We must come in humility before God and ask for the ministry of His Spirit, and for the grace to receive the revelation of truth with which He will assuredly come. His coming may well include an exposé of our condition and need, but will, with that, also include a revelation of the glory, majesty, and sovereignty of God the Father and our Lord Jesus Christ, a revelation that will *"convict the world of guilt in regard to sin and righteousness and judgment"* (John 16:8). If we have grieved or quenched the Holy Spirit we will have to repent it, certainly as individuals and even corporately, for it is impossible to serve God properly without Him.

The serious acceleration into political and public acceptance of gross sin such as we are presently witnessing in our society and culture will not be successfully faced by leaders and churches rendered fearful of the moving of the Spirit by self-seeking excess, neglect of God's word, and lack of direct witness. A retreat into sophisticated engagement with semi-religious and secular interests for the sake of a popular profile cannot be the Church's focus if she is to receive *"a kingdom that cannot be shaken . . . be thankful, and so worship God acceptably with reverence and awe"* (Hebrews 12:28). At any time this would be quite wrong, at this particular time it would be disastrous. Fathers must stir their sons. This is a moment of consequence. A new generation must know their God and their calling, be roused to life, and come before the Lord of all the earth to have their eyes opened.

Listen to the prophetic father:

> *"When the servant of the man of God got up and went out early the next morning, an army with horses and chariots had surrounded the city. 'Oh, my lord, what shall we do?' the servant asked. 'Don't be afraid,' the prophet answered. 'Those who are with us are more than those who are with them.' And Elisha prayed, 'O Lord, open his eyes so that he may see.' Then the Lord opened the servant's eyes, and he looked and saw the hills full of horses and chariots of fire all round Elisha."*

> (2 Kings 6:15–17)

We desperately need the Holy Spirit's person, presence, and power if the awesome sovereignty of God is to be felt among us and among the people. There is a very great need for the fear of the Lord of love to quicken us. This will take place only by His word and His Spirit, and we must hear the fathers who will say so.

Notes

1. That is why life in the Spirit now, though not full (not full in the same way as it was for Adam due to sinful human nature), always surprises us.
2. Reginald Heber 1783–1826, *Redemption Hymnal* (1960 ed.), No. 113.
3. I can hear Barney Coombs now, as we walked to an evening celebration together, asking the rhetorical question, "Can you really imagine the apostle Paul giving a talk on 'Breaking through the 300 barrier?'"
4. I am using the word "ministry" to mean ministry of God's word. That, I believe, is a primary way of using it. I am aware that many people today, especially in the charismatic world, when they "come forward for ministry" mean something other than ministry of God's word. They may mean prayer, counseling, prophetic encouragement, "impartation" or some combination of all these, but rarely do they mean coming before Scripture, the word of God written, for illumination, understanding, admonition, rebuke, or encouragement. I am persuaded that if we prepared ourselves to come and sit under God's word written and receive its ministry, we would need to "go forward" much less for "ministry" of other kinds – though we might find ourselves making some public stand for truth, for service, for worship, or for witness.

5. James Forsyth came regularly to the church, he was a true apostolic father and often brought with him "sons" in the faith. Three of them, Jim McConnell, Eddie Taylor, and James Connelly, went on to become remarkable preachers and leaders. Jim McConnell leads Whitewell Metropolitan Tabernacle, Belfast, the largest Pentecostal church in the UK. I heard him when he was known as a "boy preacher" and he was outstanding then.

6. Don Cox, the teaching elder, taught Bible Class every Sunday afternoon and majored on the atonement and the grace of God, prophecy and Christ's return, and the person and work of the Holy Spirit.

7. *Redemption Hymnal* (1960 ed.), No. 499.

Chapter 8

Fathers and Character

What we *are* is more important than what we *do*. This would be generally acknowledged. When it actually comes down to it, however, we are much more likely, when meeting someone, to ask, "What do you do?" rather than "What are you like?" To inquire after the development of someone's character seems impertinent. It remains true nevertheless that character is of greater consequence than talent, gift, and image.

Not only is this eminently true of fathers – what they are is more important than what they do – it is fathers themselves who are often most conscious of the truth and convinced of its importance. They know that the ongoing influence and effectiveness of spiritual ministry depends, to a very high degree, upon the quality of the character through which it passes. Our words and deeds flow most successfully through the channel of a character that is being disciplined, refined, and adjusted by submission to the nature of Christ. If the inner man remains unbroken and unbridled, no matter how the outer "image" is presented, ministry cannot continue to come through to lasting effect. The great question, therefore, has to be, how is such character to be formed?

Character first

In a pragmatic age dominated by strategy, method, and personality the quiet call for the personal exercise of disciplines necessary to the formation and nourishment of spiritual disposition sounds both slow and strange. Externalism is everywhere. The loud, the brash, the immediate grasps attention quickly and creates both expectation and excitement. It may, nevertheless, prove to be less fulfilling in the long term. By such means we might well be creating the "spiritual" equivalent of the worldly demand for instant sensation and satisfaction, a satisfaction short lived because the stimulant is essentially external and sensual and becomes an end in itself. Detached from "the bread of life" that passes into us and, by understanding, renews the mind and transforms the life, external stimulants must be constantly "taken" to the eventual dependence of the "addict." In the process we become less conscious of the inner man and the inner life, less able to engage with the disciplines of personal spiritual reality, and strangers to the inner journey. It is, nevertheless, the inner journey that remains central to the formation of character. And it is the inner path, though not well worn, that is more likely to be known by fathers. Because of this they tend to "walk" unhurriedly, are less affected by excitements and sensations, and appear to breathe a lighter air. This, perhaps, may be a reason for our slow recognition and acceptance of fathers over recent years – and a reason why, now, we are crying out for them.

We may find in a true father what Richard Foster calls a "devotional master,"[1] someone who has paid attention to the inner life, to the world within, and disciplined himself in personal devotion to Christ. We seriously need such fathers and mothers. The godliness that emanates from them will enrich and deepen our lives because it is both costly and rare. A deep and rich life invites contemplation, something for which a hurrying world finds little time.

A photograph age

When looking at a photograph I can appreciate any talent that it shows in arrangement, or skill with light and shade. But how different it is when faced with a great painting. With a great painting there is immeasurably more for the artist himself is there, his time, his thought, his feelings and fears, his loves and joys. He has poured himself into what he has done, there is a unique extension of his perception and thought in his work, in its composition and its color. A great painting, therefore, is unique and cannot be reproduced. It is rich in life and labor, there is cost and depth in it, and a cursory glance will not do. I could simply note it as I pass through the gallery of course, but I will not be enriched myself by anything less than contemplation and for that I will have to stop and look and think.

Spiritually speaking I am afraid we live in a photograph age. A thousand images a day pass swiftly before our eyes, some with momentary pleasure. But the great pictures hang quietly, unique and full, and the riches beyond the immediate impression can only be discerned and savored slowly by personal contemplation. The great characters of Scripture are like this, and the great doctrines too – together with those among us today who are godly. All alike release their riches gently to those who will stop and spend time in their presence.[2]

In my first church there was a remarkable woman. I am trying not to use the expression "little old lady" but, in fact, she was small and she was elderly. She was not a leader, nor was she prominent in any notable manner, but her presence in any gathering "deepened" it. Her prayers were quiet and released fragrance. When she said, "O God ...," the words seemed to come from where the rest of us had not been. I was inexperienced, zealous and brimful of ideas, sure of doctrine and full of words. Mrs Benson was merciful to a pastor young enough to be her son and would say to me gently from time to time, "It's the secret place, find the secret place ..." I had had two encounters with God up to that time that were significant and I knew there was such "a place," but I couldn't find the path – and I was busy! But I knew that she knew. She was a spiritual mother. Since those days, through failure, weakness and wounds, I have stumbled by grace and faith upon the path and tried to walk it. Mrs Benson, however, had found it, explored it, knew it, and like Enoch, walked with God.

In the matter of spiritual development we have been told, particularly in recent years, that everything must be done "in relationship" with others, the inference being that personal private devotion and development is somehow odd or even suspect. Having already looked at relationships a little you will not be surprised at my gently questioning this inference. Personal self-enquiry and self-discipline are essential elements in the formation of character, they set our true and inner affections on Christ and enlarge the place of His dwelling. To be sure, we seek the inner path as fellow travelers in the community of faith and as members of Christ's body. It is vital that we do so for a number of reasons, and for this one at least, that, if as members of Christ we fail to pursue and possess some measure of reality in the inner life, the church itself (for the church is us) will eventually lack depth, become superficial, and be laid low by obsession with the external and the sensual. Nevertheless, fathers and mentors know that all spiritual life and reality is located in Christ in the private sanctum of the inner man. God longs that we find in Him the overwhelming fullness for which He made us, the all-sustaining life, light, and love that alone *"satisfies the thirsty and fills the hungry with good things"* (Psalm 107:9). "This intercourse between God and the soul is known to us in conscious personal awareness. It is personal: that is, it does not come through the body of believers as such, but is known to the individual, and to the body through the individuals which compose it."[3] In an age well nigh suffocating under the demands made by an unbalanced philosophy of external communalism we must seek a better relationship between individual and corporate spirituality.

Submission to the nature of Christ

This much, therefore, we must say: Godly character is formed by personal and private submission to the nature of Christ in the inner life.[4] As the Holy Spirit commends to us through God's word various elements of the divine nature born in us, we may choose to submit to those elements as we meet circumstances in our daily lives that call for them.

So, for example, our pride surrenders to His humility, our aggression to His meekness, our excess to His temperance and purity, our sullenness to His joy. The state and progress of this inward formation and development is not always apparent outwardly. Skills and talents can hide, sometimes for a long period, an ill-formed character, especially if those skills and talents operate publicly and are honed to a high level of platform performance. People may then be moved by what we do rather than formed by what we are. Instead of making disciples, we create fans.

A true spiritual father ministers to his sons through his person rather than his performance, by his life rather than his talent. For this to take place there has to be a measure of close personal fellowship and it is in such fellowship that any gap between his public charisma and personal character is reduced. What he *is* reaches through his public gifts and skills to strengthen, encourage, and guide us. If the major spiritual influences upon us are dominant yet remote public figures with powerful ministries and images we will not become sons. Fathers run the risk of personal fellowship. There is no other way to "beget" sons and make them into servants.

It is often when we pause to ask ourselves how a spiritual father affects us, how we feel after he has been with us, what his presence means to us, that the matter becomes clear – what he is takes precedence over what he does.

Here, then, are some things that spiritual fathers are:

▶ **Fathers are stable and constant**. Faith and experience have matured and settled them so that when they are around we feel safe, their presence creates a sense of security. This kind of stability grows out of peace with God, a position of acceptance based on the removal of accusation and the divine declaration of pardon. A legal position brought about through Christ's death and resurrection upon which a personal experience of assurance, even full assurance, may be established. Here is the one true and solid ground for stability and constancy.

▶ **Fathers are prudent**. Their knowledge and assessment of life's circumstances make them wary of quick solutions. They will often take time over answers and even then appear to come to a matter by a roundabout route. The truth is that discretion looks at things from various perspectives and takes into account factors that others miss. The process is sometimes dismissed as lacking faith but this is rarely the case with true fathers. Prudence and discretion should be welcomed as a major contribution to sound judgment. The phrase "my son" is used in Proverbs twenty-three times, predominantly in the context of a father's wisdom and prudence (particularly in the face of sexual temptation), for example,

> *"My son, keep my words*
> *and store up my commands within you.*
> *Keep my commands and you will live;*
> *guard my teachings as the apple of your eye."*

(Proverbs 7:1–2)

▶ **Fathers are straightforward**. Though often cautious in deliberation over situations, their eventual judgment is clear. When more immediate action is called for fathers can be direct and forthright, sometimes disconcertingly so. My father had an annoying habit of knowing when my brothers and I were "flying a kite" – putting up a test flight to see which way the wind would blow in the event of a serious take off. It rarely worked, and even when it did I suspect he knew what we were doing all along. His normal response – after letting us talk ourselves out of breath – was to put an unerring finger on the nub of the matter, usually with an uncomplicated negative!

▶ **Fathers are substantial**. There is nothing flimsy about fathers, all is solid and sound. This is the result of a ministry that has worked through issues, applied truth and doctrine to many circumstances and questions, and lived with the consequences whether easy or difficult. In what is often a superficial and image-dominated culture, even in church life, the idea of substance and weight can be thought "heavy." We simply have to say that it isn't, that we are tired of phony fair-weather hype, and would gladly exchange it for some robust realism and durable quality.

A situation arose in a church overseas with which we were connected. It was a young church, planted and sustained by strong ministries. The main body of the church was made up of younger adults, couples, and families. This was quite natural because the leaders were young and enthusiastic, full of praise, faith, and music. Many of the young people and some of the couples visited Manna Christian Fellowship in Maidstone and blessed us with their zeal and joy in Christ. During their visit they made an interesting observation: "Your church," they said, "feels substantial and secure. You have people who know God in a deep way, who have known Him for a long time and have proved His word. We have few like this. We are children. What can we do?" The situation became more difficult for them when the leaders, following the directing of the Spirit, moved on to another city, appointing a very good but somewhat inexperienced young man in their place.

At this time a mature couple from one of our churches, good spiritual "parents" of worth and substance, were led by the Spirit to move from Maidstone to live and fellowship with the young church. Released by our leadership to this ministry they brought experience, security, and affirmation to the younger believers over a number of years and made a lasting contribution to the growth of that church. It is worthy of note that, while used by God prophetically, they possessed little in the way of platform speaking gifts and skills – their ministry lay in what they were, experienced, stable, substantial, and prudent.

► **Fathers are balanced**. They are able to see the wider picture, take into account what others would ignore as peripheral, and weigh up issues. Because of this it is difficult to get fathers to take up extreme positions, they have learned to be steady, to keep their doctrinal, spiritual, and emotional equilibrium. Some people will see this as lack of decision, of sitting on the fence. This is rarely the case with fathers and mentors: they know that momentum requires balance.

The Pentecostal teacher, author, and spiritual statesman, Donald Gee (later Principal of the Assemblies of God Bible School in the UK), was often called the "apostle of balance." Unhappily there were those who used the term to suggest that he compromised the Pentecostal message. Nothing could have been further from the truth. Donald Gee simply would not allow himself to be pushed into extreme positions. He believed that it would deny him the opportunity to speak to the many church leaders from mainstream denominations who came to him for understanding. His books became worldwide classics on Pentecostal themes, his editorship of *Pentecost*, a magazine commissioned by the World Pentecostal Conference, was unique, and his leadership of the Assemblies of God Bible School renowned. Lack of passion because balanced? I think not. I saw and heard him profoundly moved with gratitude to God for the Pentecostal message as it came of age, and he was sometimes overwhelmed with happiness because of the leaders and churches who looked to him for his unique combination of devotion and dignity, enthusiasm and courtesy.

► **Fathers are wide thinking**. They are neither narrow of mind nor thin in experience. To spend time with a pinched and narrow mind is limiting and uncomfortable; there is no potential for expansion in it, no love of freedom, no light of discovery; all is tram-lined, decided, restricted. True spiritual fathers have the light of life in their eyes; they have space around them and horizons before them. Young men like to be with them because there is the possibility of a fresh perspective, a different angle, a breadth of discussion. A father will encourage us to think: "Use your mind," he will say. "God gave it you. Engage your intellect;

consider possibilities; study, read, reflect, contemplate. Let the wind of the Spirit blow through your thinking, open the windows of your wits to God, love and worship the Lord with all your mind."

The apostle Paul had breadth. The Psalmist said, *"How precious to me are your thoughts, O God. How vast is the sum of them!"* (Psalm 139:17), and to that vastness of divine thought Paul dared to open his mind – and the mind of his sons. No wonder he declared, when the overwhelming glory of revelation gave him a glimpse of the divine span beyond natural comprehension and he realized that all was wider and larger than he had ever imagined:

> *"Oh, the depth of the riches of the wisdom and*
> *knowledge of God!*
> *How unsearchable his judgments,*
> *and his paths beyond tracing out!*
> *'Who has known the mind of the Lord?*
> *Or who has been his counselor?'*
> *'Who has ever given to God,*
> *that God should repay him?'*
> *For from him and through him and to him are all things.*
> *To him be the glory forever! Amen."* (Romans 11:33–36)

Paul's prayer for the believers at Ephesus was in similar vein. Anything but narrow-minded, it reflected the sunlit panorama of his own illuminated intellect:

> *"I keep asking that the God of our Lord Jesus Christ, the glorious Father, may give you the Spirit of wisdom and revelation, so that you may know him better. I pray also that the eyes of your heart may be enlightened in order that you may know the hope to which he has called you, the riches of his glorious inheritance in the saints, and his incomparably great power for us who believe."*
> (Ephesians 1:17–19)

Here is the true spiritual father's prayer. Here is his desire for his spiritual children, to see them loosed from the narrow agendas of sectarian and institutional bondage, whether liberal, charismatic, mystic or evangelical (for that can be as sectarian as the rest),[5] into the glorious breadth of Scripture wherein is revealed, by His Spirit, the sovereign God Himself.

▶ **Fathers are joyful and cheerful**. It is quite wrong to equate sound substance and prudent wisdom with cheerless gravity. The very opposite ought to be true. Surely solid ground and a good understanding are the very foundations necessary for joy and cheerfulness? The idea that Scripture, doctrine, exposition, theology and holy living are all gloom and solemnity is wrong. I would resent the idea except that resentment makes one miserable! And where does this wretched idea come from? I have good reason to believe that it comes from the devil (John 10:10). No, spiritual fathers have the best of all reasons for being cheerful.

It is often a father's *"cheerful heart"* that is *"good medicine"* (Proverbs 17:22) to bless a careworn leader; he will often be like a "spread table," an "anointed head," and an "overflowing cup" (cf. Psalm 23:5), even in the presence of enemies. Through a spiritual father and wise mentor God's truth will lift the mind and heart, and God's Spirit anoint with the *"oil of gladness instead of mourning, and a garment of praise instead of a spirit of despair"* (Isaiah 61:3; see also Psalm 104:15 and Hebrews 1:9).[6]

There is a deal too much super-spirituality about: it has no carefree joy, is humorless, intense, always trying – and makes everyone uncomfortable. It isn't cheerful, and fathers dislike it. The reason for its not being cheerful, basically, is because it's always "on the hunt" for something wrong, something bad, or something more. Fathers, in happy contrast, encourage us with the fullness and freedom that we have *already* been given and graced with in Christ, and in that good knowledge cheer us on increasingly to possess, appreciate, and enjoy it.

One thing more. Because sin ruins everything but God, fatherhood also suffers its ruin, as briefly outlined in our opening chapters. This means that many people have known only cheerless, broken, and sometimes unkind fathers. The image and reality of true fatherhood, with all its happy pleasure and delight, has been ruined by sin so that it has become a bruised and bruising travesty. To be sure, this does not mean that all fathers are bad and cheerless. By common grace multitudes have been all that they could be – but that is not true for everyone. How incredibly wonderful, then, is the gospel of God, that through Christ restores all things, including fatherhood, and by faith gives us sight and sound of our heavenly home, our heavenly family, and our heavenly Father.

"Watch your life and your ministry"

Because character takes priority over gift it does not mean that gift is unimportant. It's a matter of proportion and balance. Paul said to Timothy, *"Watch your life **and** doctrine closely"* (1 Timothy 4:16, my emphasis): both were important. Fathers will exemplify this as well as encourage it. They know that "successful" ministry flows best through a character that is being formed by submission to the nature of Christ.

As we understand the priority of a father's character, we may proceed in the next chapter to identify some of the things that fathers and mentors do.

Notes

1. *Celebration of Discipline* (Hodder & Stoughton, 1999, new edn), p. 145. This book remains one of the truly great classics of spiritual devotion, a book among books.
2. Sometimes when studying I feel my mind slow before some great truth. I stop writing, still myself, think, and sense some greatness move before "my eyes." I have learned in these moments that, if I seek to bring my mind to worship, I will begin to "see" something. Disjointed ideas, text, thoughts, like so many colors and shapes, begin to resolve themselves into harmony and form, and I find myself looking, slowly, into the living heart of a doctrine, into its depths and riches, into its reality and substance. By an exquisite illumination I may, for a long moment, see into some wondrous part of the eternal knowing. For me these are among the richest of all times, almost impossible to recapture, though sometimes a knowing remains. If such a moment returns to you while preaching, however, you will know the meaning of unction and ecstasy of expression.
3. A.W. Tozer, *The Pursuit of God* (Lakeland Christian Publications Inc., 1948), p. 14.
4. This is not a book on the development of the inner life but it is impossible not to give some emphasis to its necessity seeing as it will always be a major focus in the ministry of spiritual fathers.
5. Please don't misunderstand me. I am profoundly grateful for those movements that have sought by all manner of means to preserve and proclaim what would generally be called evangelical doctrine or the doctrines of God's grace. Nevertheless, be the label evangelical, charismatic, or liberal, it cannot be used to mean that thinking of that kind will never become hidebound. A narrow evangelical mind is as closed as any other.
6. In these references oil, a symbol of the Holy Spirit, is used in connection with joy and gladness. The Spirit's anointing upon us, therefore, cheers and gladdens the heart.

Chapter 9

What Fathers Do

My father seemed to be good at so many things. Growing vegetables, mending bicycles, repairing shoes, plumbing closets, and hanging wallpaper were just some of them. On shoe-repair night I was allowed to hold the blacking stick over the gas flame until it was soft enough to apply to the edge of the new sole. And when Dad was decorating it was my job to mark the paper as he placed it against the wall, and cut it with scissors too big for my fingers. Today Pat sometimes says to me, "At least you can hang wallpaper." I wonder why? And no, I don't repair shoes or grow vegetables. But Summer Saturdays spent with my brothers on Dad's vegetable allotment seem, now, to have been all warm sunshine and humming crickets, with sandwiches brought over by mother in the afternoon and tea on the ground behind the redcurrant bushes. And there was the public pump. We always soaked ourselves at the pump before the day was done.

Fathers "form" us

We come, then, to consider what fathers do. Before looking, however, at some of the specific things, it would be best, first, to identify the general and overall function of fathers toward their children. In this wide and all-embracing sense their "ministry" is simple enough to state, though truly profound in process – fathers "form" us. We hear what they think, we watch what they do, we learn what they teach, we copy what they show. By all these things fathers form us in mind and life, and when we in our turn follow our fathers (for following is essential to forming), they affirm our best efforts and correct our bad ones. And when necessary they help us pick up the pieces. By such mentoring fathers shape and fashion us: we develop ideas and patterns of thought, become willing to watch, listen and learn, and match the encouragement to do it ourselves with the pluck to make the effort, even at the risk of failure. We know that our father is there for us.

This central idea of spiritual formation is born out in the words of concern written by the apostle Paul to the Galatians:

> *"My dear children, for whom I am again in the pains of childbirth until Christ is **formed** in you . . . "*
> (Galatians 4:19, my emphasis)

Paul clearly saw fathering in terms of spiritual formation, of relating and ministering to his children in Christ in such a way as to promote the development of Christ's character in them. Underlying all the care and guidance, all the encouragement and example, was this fundamental purpose, this exceedingly wonderful purpose, of seeing Christ formed in his spiritual children. In the case of the Galatians Paul was in considerable distress because the basic elements of that formation had been interfered with and he felt himself *"in the pains of childbirth"* for them again.

This, then, is what spiritual fathers do: they form "Christ" in their children, laboring and looking for the gradual development of Christ's disposition in their lives. It is what Paul had in mind when he said to the Corinthians,

> *"... in Christ Jesus I became your father through the gospel. Therefore I urge you to imitate me."* (1 Corinthians 4:15–16)

Not that Paul might reproduce himself in them, but that Christ might be formed in them as He was in Paul.

It is here, in this unique truth of Christ's nature and image being formed in us, that we come face to face with the divine and age-long purpose of the Christian ministry in all its aspects: that *"those God foreknew he also predestined to **be conformed to the likeness of his Son**, that he might be the firstborn among many brothers"* (Romans 8:29, my emphasis). All our preaching, planting, and prophesying, our evangelizing and mission, our pastoring, teaching, and fathering is to this astonishing and glorious beginning and ending: the honor, praise, and pleasure of the Father in forming the likeness of His beloved Son in His entire family,

> *"For he chose us in him* [Christ] *before the creation of the world to be holy and blameless in his sight. In love he predestined us to be adopted as his sons through Jesus Christ, in accordance with his pleasure and will – to the praise of his glorious grace, which he has freely given us in the One he loves."*   (Ephesians 1:4–6)

Paul had glimpsed the glory of this divine purpose and therefore defined the Christian ministry in his letter to the Colossians in the following statement as:

> *" . . . the mystery that has been kept hidden for ages and generations, but is now disclosed to the saints. To them God has chosen to make known among the Gentiles the glorious riches of this mystery, which is Christ in you,* **the hope of glory***. We proclaim him, admonishing and teaching everyone with all wisdom,* **so that we may present everyone perfect in Christ***. To this end I labor, struggling with all his energy, which so powerfully works in me."*   (Colossians 1:26–29, my emphasis)

Here is the sum and substance of a true spiritual father's work and ministry, to *"present everyone perfect in Christ,"* to see Christ so formed in every child of God, so conformed to the family likeness and image that the heart of *the* Father overflows with paternal pleasure and fills all the unending ages with joy:

> *"The L*ORD *your God is with you,*
>   *he is mighty to save.*
> *He will take great delight in you,*
>   *he will quiet you with his love,*
>   *he will rejoice over you with singing."*   (Zephaniah 3:17)

What fathers do to form Christ in us

Fathers care
A father's heart fills with affection and interest when faced with the concerns of his children. He cannot help it. He is caught

up in their feelings, in their desires and ambitions, their joys, disappointments, and hurts. He will commiserate, cry, and laugh with them. Why? Because, quite simply, he cares.

A father will be moved by the heartache or joy of his child – and it will not matter how young or old the child is. Tears will fill his eyes as he thinks of the years a son has wasted or the hard road a daughter has chosen for herself. He will rejoice with a friend whose child has done well, while his own heart cries for the child he has lost. His caring heart will sing for the daughter who steps up for her degree, for the son who overcomes at great cost one more hurdle on the road to normality, for the "child" promoted to management, and the other who displays the most remarkable grit and courage in the face of trouble.

The apostle Paul, after listing in 2 Corinthians 11 the astonishing catalogue of physical trials through which he had passed for the sake of the gospel, went on to say,

> *"Besides everything else, I face daily the pressure of my concern for all the churches. Who is weak, and I do not feel weak? Who is led into sin, and I do not inwardly burn?"*
>
> (2 Corinthians 11:28–29)

Such was Paul's care for the churches that he found in himself an empathy that somehow "included" him in the sufferings, and sins, of others.

Fathers do not always know how much they care until circumstances overtake them. The telephone in my study rang and I answered it to hear a friend, an apostolic leader in Europe, on the other end. Did I have time to listen? Of course. His usually cheerful voice, full of fun and faith, was broken with tears. A crisis in his team was imminent, meetings and dialogue (including my own counsel) had availed nothing. What was he to do? The church would have to be informed that week. His weeping filled my ears and my heart.

At the same time, in a Manchester hospital, my mother lay close to death. What in all the world should I do? "Keep trusting," I said. "I'll be on a plane in the morning." And then, when he was gone, "Dear God, please keep mother with us until I get back." It was a heart-rending four days, days of deep hurt, compassion, comfort, and prayer. I flew home at the end of the week and drove straight to Manchester from the airport to be with mother, who *was* still with us. A few days later I sat with her as she died.

Fathers listen

To have someone who actually listens is rare. Most people are simply waiting for us to draw breath so that they can say "I know," before going on to recount a similar experience of their own. This is especially true with illnesses or trouble. We have hardly finished telling our own story before the "listener" is saying, "I know, I know, it was the same for me ...," but of course it wasn't, it was worse! Most of us are like this.

In order to listen well we must find in our heart a true interest in the person who wants to talk. Listening, therefore, is born out of care. I have learned a good deal in this respect from my friend and ministry colleague Andrew Parfitt. He believes that a principle of true fellowship and ministry is contained in Paul's words to the Philippians,

> *"Each of you should look not only to your own interests, but also to the interests of others."* (Philippians 2:4)

The principle has become part of his own life so that he is genuinely interested in the concerns, plans, and dreams of other people. He is therefore happy to listen without having to suppress a craving to talk about himself.[1] This gracious ability lies, with others, at the heart of successful pastoring; it is certainly a chief characteristic of spiritual fathers and mentors. An obsession with our own interests and opinions invites little confidence because it has no ear for others. *"Nobody,"* said Paul, *"should seek his own good, but the good of others"* (1 Corinthians 10:24). He commended Timothy in the following words,

> *"I have no one else like him, who takes a genuine interest in your welfare. For everyone looks out for his own interests, not those of Jesus Christ."* (Philippians 2:20–21)

To know that we are being heard and taken seriously is uplifting. Loving attention is a precious thing. In any conversation regarding spiritual fathers it will be said, sooner or later, that, "It's his willingness to listen that I so much appreciate."

Often, when I answer the phone and hear a leader on the other end, I prepare my heart to listen. It isn't always required, but more often than not it is – though sometimes the desire to be heard is not immediately expressed. A few questions, a comment or two and some information, and then a hesitant pause: "Was there something else?" I ask. "Well, do you have a few moments?" And then I'm listening. I am grateful to God for a listening heart but there have been many times when I've missed the signals, times when I should have caught the note of longing for my ear but was too preoccupied with other things. Often we are moving too quickly to hear the unspoken, "Please, listen to me."

It would be wrong, however, to suppose that a father's listening ear is always being filled with troubles. Very often it is simply spiritual father and son sharing the everyday life of ministry, forgetting their respective roles (and ages) in the pleasure of fellowship and stimulating conversation, and the mutual enjoyment of walking with each other through truth, doctrine, and holy history, a history to which they themselves are making an almost unconscious addition as they worship and work together. We must never underestimate the value of simple friendship, of just spending time with each other.

Fathers give time

Caring and listening means time. There is no way around this. There are no substitutes for time, and giving it will often mean sacrifice somewhere. Leaders sometimes unconsciously (and, alas, sometimes consciously) feel that they must carry an air of busyness, appear always purposeful, and wear a slightly preoccupied look that says, "I am God's servant, try not to bother me." Spiritual fathers have usually come to terms with this tendency, taken themselves in hand, found grace, slowed down, and set their agenda to give time.

I have a memory tucked away in my personal archives. It is simple enough, but moving. A number of years ago I overheard a mother and her little boy in conversation about his being met at the school gates at the end of the day. The mother was explaining why she could not be there and that someone else, a friend, would meet him. The lad was not happy. "You'll be alright," she said, "and I'll leave you some money." I have never forgotten his reply. "I don't want money," he said. "I want you."

Once we begin to understand the worth of people, giving time falls into place. It is part of a father's heart to know this worth and it is this knowing that enables him to see beyond self-interest and make time. The issue is not, "Will this enhance my reputation?" or, "Will this be noticed by others?" The issue is the value of the person (not even any response that the person might make). A spiritual father knows that if he is to invest his life in his children it will take time. Time, in this case, is not to be calculated. It is the gift of love.

My friend Tim Simpson said to me, "I really love walking with people through their hurts and problems. Usually I don't have answers, but I can be with them." That is a true father's heart. I minister into Tim's church regularly and I know just how much the people love him. He sometimes shares doubts with me about the worth and success of his ministry. The truth is he ministers to Christ through compassion for his people. I am not sure how that is measured on the success charts but it certainly makes for real church.

Fathers share weight

Caring, listening, and giving time will inevitably mean sharing weight. The problems, hurts, responsibilities, and duties of ministry can be heavy. Spiritual fathers, together with the giving of care and time, are also able to carry weight. Their shoulders are strong to support burdens and, by so doing, relieve sons for whom the weight has become overwhelming. The Pharisees angered Jesus because they did the exact opposite to this: *"you experts in the law,"* He said, *"woe to you, because you load people down with burdens they can hardly carry, and you yourselves will not lift one finger to help them"* (Luke 11:46).

Fathers and mentors know that very often a desire for time and talk means that ministry has become heavy and they are probably being called to share it. Paul knew this experience well,

> *"We who are strong ought to bear with the failings of the weak and not to please ourselves."* (Romans 15:1)

> *"Carry each other's burdens, and in this way . . . fulfil the law of Christ."* (Galatians 6:2)

That law was expressed in Jesus' lovely words to the people in Matthew 11:28–30, people worn and weighed down by the religious teachers of the day:

"Come to me, all you who are weary and burdened, and I will give you rest. Take my yoke upon you and learn from me, for I am gentle and humble in heart, and you will find rest for your souls. For my yoke is easy and my burden is light."

Fathers and mentors know that sons are not best formed by the crushing weight of man-made religious expectations, but by the yoke and burden of Christ,[2] which matches responsibility with rest for our souls.

Fathers release

We will look elsewhere in these chapters at the need for letting sons go. It is enough to say here that spiritual fathers have to resist the temptation to make their "children" dependent upon them. The great joy of fathering is to see Christ so formed in each one that they know and walk with God in their own right. We must not create for ourselves an immature clientele who know God only in us, who filter all their understanding, choices, and decisions through us, and have no desire for the wind under their own wings. It may not be easy, for any number of reasons, but we must teach our sons to fly.

It is at this point, too, that we begin to understand the times and seasons connected with fathering, both for leaders and churches. We cannot afford to miss the season for release, the time to let go. If we do miss it our fathering may become an embarrassment, and even a hindrance.

In a statement to His disciples that they found extremely difficult, Jesus said,

"I tell you the truth: It is for your good that I am going away. Unless I go away, the Counselor will not come to you; but if I go, I will send him to you." (John 16:7)

The future ministry of Jesus *through* them could only be brought to fruition by the end of His ministry *among* them.

A final note

As already seen, forming Christ in sons calls for an authentic ministry of the word of Scripture: that ministry is central to all spiritual formation and transformation. However, the qualities of loving care and time that have been considered in this chapter are essential to the success of that word ministry. Without the caring heart, the listening ear, the gift of time, the sharing of weight, and the releasing of life, the finest doctrinal understanding and expository ability will fail. Not fail so far as the truth itself is concerned, but fail in making the kind of connection that enables that truth to be heard and received.

Notes

1. I have known many people who were pastored by Andrew Parfitt's own father, T.S. Parfitt, a beloved and long-time teaching pastor of the church now led by Andrew and me. Those people talk in glowing terms of his fatherly care and sacrificial interest in their everyday lives. It is clear that Andrew was influenced deeply by his father's example and that it has found expression in his own ministry – that's fathering.

2. Christ's yoke and burden *will* disciple and train us, but they will rest and strengthen us too. The man-made burdens of "the ministry" – its expectations and demands – are not like this and we must be careful of them. We are to take "*His* yoke," "*His* burden," they will not overwhelm and crush us because they are easy and light. They are burdens, to be sure, but they are *His*.

Chapter 10

Fathers – and Sons

Sonship lies at the heart of the Christian faith. It is at once the supreme and unique means by which God reveals Himself to us – *"In the past God spoke to our forefathers through the prophets at many times and in various ways, but in these last days he has spoken to us by his Son ... "* (Hebrews 1:1–2) – and the highest position in which we ourselves stand before Him. As John exclaimed,

> *"How great is the love the Father has lavished on us, that we should be called children of God! And that is what we are!"*
>
> (1 John 3:1)

Coming now to look more particularly at the relationship between fathers and sons brings us back to the heart of the Christian faith. Having looked already at the fatherhood of God and the sonship of the Lord Jesus Christ and seen it as a touchstone of truth and doctrine, we may turn now, with those truths in mind, to the relationship between fathers and sons in the body of Christ.

Knowing sons, knowing fathers

Fathers make good their relationship to spiritual children by the manifestation of those qualities and characteristics that are the essence of spiritual fatherhood. This does not happen in every case where a preaching ministry is used by the Holy Spirit to bring people to new birth. We may, therefore, be fathers in fact but not necessarily fathers in function. It is very likely, of course, that those who come to Christ under our ministry will consider us in the initial sense to be their spiritual father. Among them, however, together with others, will be those with whom a special relationship develops. Such a relationship will not be forced or demanded, it can come about only by a divine joining of mind and heart: "The nature of a true spiritual son is not something that can be taught in a classroom. It comes by revelation and unfolds over a period of time."[1]

I wandered from my office into the church restaurant one morning, glanced around at the people enjoying their coffee and talking together, and saw a church leader that I knew but could not remember seeing there before. Walking toward him I suddenly felt within myself an anguish of heart. I greeted him, saw the hurt in his face, and knew that he and I were going to walk together. Although we already knew each other a special relationship began that morning with a revelation that God had brought us together. Peter had been "given" me to father and encourage. He has gone on to plant and pastor a fine growing church in which my ministry with him plays a part.

Paul, Timothy, and Titus

Paul spoke of Timothy with great affection as *"my son whom I love"* (1 Corinthians 4:17), revealing a bond between them without which fathering cannot work.

Paul had first met Timothy in Lystra on his second apostolic mission. Lystra had been remarkably impacted by the power of the gospel on Paul's first visit (Acts 14:6–20), but there had also been appalling persecution. He had been stoned, dragged outside the city, and left for dead. The new disciples had gathered around him and saw him revive and it is certain that the young Timothy, if not actually involved in these events, would have known the details and been affected by them. His Jewish mother Eunice was a believer as was his grandmother (2 Timothy 1:5), and he had been acquainted with Scripture from infancy (2 Timothy 3:15). *"The brothers at Lystra and Iconium spoke well of him"* (Acts 16:2), and Paul, consequently, chose him as a traveling companion, his *"true son in the faith"* (1 Timothy 1:2). Later Paul wrote to the Philippians about Timothy in glowing terms, saying that he had *"proved himself, because as **a son with his father** he has served with me in the work of the gospel"*

(Philippians 2:22, my emphasis). Writing to Timothy himself Paul called him *"my dear son"* (2 Timothy 1:2) and confessed that he longed to see him *"so that I may be filled with joy"* (2 Timothy 1:4).

Paul's relationship with Titus, while not so well documented, has about it the same kind of fatherly grace and guidance. He, too, is *"my true son in our common faith"* (Titus 1:4).

It is the framework of revelation, connection, and affection between the apostle and his "sons" that underlies and supports the wealth of teaching and guidance contained in the epistles written to them.

Some general principles in Paul's epistles to Timothy

The apostle's instruction and counsel to his son in the faith speaks to us today with remarkable clarity and force. It is contemporary in both content and concern.

Apostolic direction

Paul often gave direction to Timothy's ministry, outlining his responsibilities and giving him specific tasks to fulfill. For example in 1 Timothy 1:3 he urges him to *"stay there in Ephesus so that you may command certain men not to teach false doctrines any longer."* It was clear direction. *"Timothy, my son,"* he continued, *"I give you this instruction in keeping with the prophecies once made about you, so that by following them you may fight the good fight, holding on to faith and a good conscience"* (1 Timothy 1:18–19).

Spiritual fathers, particularly those in an apostolic role, will, in the course of mentoring their sons, direct them to carry out various tasks. They will often send them, sometimes with delegated authority, to carry out ministry and mission responsibilities:

> *"We sent Timothy, who is our brother and God's fellow-worker in spreading the gospel of Christ, to strengthen and encourage you in your faith ..."* (1 Thessalonians 3:2)

By receiving direction and instruction willingly sons learn to bear responsibility, fulfill obligations, and discharge duties. Trusting sons with responsibility is a primary characteristic of true fathering. Those who will not take such risks (and the risks are real), who trust no one but themselves to fulfill ministry, and hold the reins of service and position too tightly to themselves, will lack both sons and successors and cannot properly be called spiritual fathers. Those who honor their sons with trust will find in them an affection that will lend both attention and pleasure to obedience and duty.

Instruction and direction, therefore, lies central to discipleship. An apprentice is not simply told *about* his work, he is given instruction, example, and experience in actually doing it, with direction on when and where to carry it out. Fathers sometimes find it necessary to point out to churches and leaders that they are too high on information and too low on instruction, that is, they are rich in knowledge but poor in action. If sons are to learn and grow, they will need to be given direction and responsibility.

There is, however, a problem here. It is possible to take these and other elements of discipleship and, in a desire for success, do what we so often do, turn them into a process: write manuals, engage experts, run classes, and "produce disciples" by means of an almost systematic procedure. It will not work. Simply taking the mechanics of discipleship without the revelation, the spiritual joining, the love, will create adherents (with the possibility of unhappy disaffection later), rather than growing, maturing sons.

Philosophical controversy

Did Timothy have a tendency to get embroiled in side issues? There is a certain insistence in Paul's counsel to him along these lines. *"Have nothing to do,"* he says, *"with godless myths and old wives' tales ..."* (1 Timothy 4:7), *"turn away from godless chatter ..."* (1 Timothy 6:20), and avoid *"foolish and stupid arguments, because you know they produce quarrels"* (2 Timothy 2:23).

Paul's general answer to this kind of thing was *"sound doctrine"* (1 Timothy 1:10; 2 Timothy 4:3). By this he meant the sum and substance of truths clearly revealed in Scripture to be fundamental elements of the gospel, properly interpreted, understood and compared, and held as a cohesive and authoritative body of belief. His instruction to Timothy to study, hold, and teach *"sound doctrine"* was given against the background of an increasing tendency in certain believers (of which Paul was well aware) to turn away from biblical foundations due to a fascination for new ideas and a taste for novelty.

Today's generation of sons must heed Paul's apostolic fathering. We are living at a time when obsession for "new" things, in every field, ignores history and wisdom, and flies in the face of wise judgment. In 2 Timothy 4:3–4 we read:

> *"For the time will come when men will not put up with sound doctrine. Instead, to suit their own desires, they will gather around them a great number of teachers to say what their itching ears want to hear. They will turn their ears away from the truth and turn aside to myths."*

This prophetic warning has been fulfilled time and again among the churches in subsequent years since Paul gave it. It is especially true today and spiritual fathers will not be slow to underline the apostle's clear-sighted counsel.

Certainly the contemporary pursuit of the new and novel has tended to relegate essentials of the gospel to optional status, elevated minor ideas into main-plank "doctrines," and reduced divine prohibitions to mere cultural shibboleths. Retrospective repentance, generational confession, feminist replacement, homosexual partnership, and church deconstruction combine to rewrite the New Testament in order to accommodate the political and social correctness of a neo-evangelicalism infatuated with tolerance and broad-mindedness. Spiritual fathers and mentors will stand in Paul's "apostolic succession" (and Paul himself served in what was thought to be a sophisticated and "relevant new world") and call their sons to expound with clarity, grace, and vigor *"the trustworthy message"* and *"sound doctrine"* commended to Timothy and Titus (Titus 1:9). We may engage the ideas of our time with spiritual insight, biblical integrity, and plain language, without being "holy" or heavy, or descending into a tangled mass of endless argument and religious psychobabble.[2]

Confirming prophecies

All prophetic words and messages should be weighed and received, or set aside (and sometimes rejected), accordingly (1 Corinthians 14:29). The prophetic word spoken to the young Timothy seems to have identified a gift bestowed upon him by the Lord when the elders of the churches at Lystra and Iconium, together with Paul, laid hands on him and released him into ministry (1 Timothy 4:14; 2 Timothy 1:6). Clearly the apostle, now, sees a need for the prophecy to be recalled and confirmed. He writes, therefore,

> *"Timothy, my son, I give you this instruction* **in keeping with** *the prophecies once made about you, so that by following them you may fight the good fight."*   (1 Timothy 1:18, my emphasis)

Notwithstanding the thousands of unweighed "words" running loose in the Christian world (and thousands of unaccountable word-givers too), spiritual fathers will continue to encourage us to value the gift of prophecy (cf. 1 Corinthians 14:39; 1 Thessalonians 5:19–21). They will help us maintain a proper balance between the written word and the prophetic word, and persuade us to bring the prophetic word before Scripture for verification and validation. To share with a wise and mature father a prophetic word that has been given us is not a slight upon the one who prophesied. It is a good thing to do – and may be very reassuring. At some later time, when we find ourselves passing through a difficult period in our life or ministry, our father may feel it necessary to remind us of what the Holy Spirit said and encourage us to stir ourselves again because of it.

Spiritual warfare

Following the affirmation of Timothy's gift and the prophecy that accompanied it, Paul went on to exhort his son to *"fight the good fight, holding on to faith and a good conscience"* (1 Timothy 1:18–19). He was saying in effect, "The prophetic word *was* real, there *is* divinely bestowed gift in you, encourage yourself, this is the time to be strong, to fight for truth and faith. You know this is your calling, Timothy. Keep your conscience clear by fulfilling it."

Reading through the two letters Paul wrote to the young leader reveals a father's love and encouragement for a son who may have been prone to fits of doubt and discouragement. The apostle, therefore, urges him on:

> *"For this reason I remind you to fan into flame the gift of God, which is in you through the laying on of my hands."*
>
> (2 Timothy 1:6)

There is the same note again. Stir up the divine deposit, don't rely on your own natural assets, rouse the gift of God in your life so that you can *"fight the good fight of the faith"* (1 Timothy 6:12).

In Timothy's case the fight was for truth, doctrine, and the quality of his inner life. This is still, today, the major battle-ground. Paul exhorts Timothy to overcome the enemy in his own mind and heart – *"Watch your life and doctrine closely"* (1 Timothy 4:16) – and so take his confidence into the public arena and *"not be ashamed to testify about our Lord, or ashamed of me his prisoner. But join with me in suffering for the gospel, by the power of God"* (2 Timothy 1:8). It is a moving appeal from an apostolic father's heart. Timothy needed it, and so do we.

Personal diligence

All fathers know that diligence, hard work, and perseverance are integral to success. Paul has no compunction, therefore, as we have seen, in calling upon Timothy to join him in enduring hardship. *"Join with me,"* he says, *"in suffering for the gospel . . . "* (2 Timothy 1:8).

This is a recurring theme throughout the two letters. Paul obviously sees the need to encourage Timothy to be diligent and dedicated, both in his personal life and in his ministry. There will be difficult times, there will be uncomfortable issues, there will be battles. Ministry does bring great spiritual victory and blessed deliverance, but those very blessings imply conflict, endurance, and the trial of faith.

I am aware that in this respect fathers and mentors will sometimes be thought rather negative, obsessed, perhaps, with dogged perseverance and fortitude. Of course, when young men are rejoicing together in their calling and ministry, in their vision and faith, when they are prophesying to one another with cheerful and carefree confidence, it is not the best time for sober and experience-laden reminders of trial and trouble ahead. Wise fathers will look for the balance between lively confidence in God's word, and robust diligence in the face of hardship and opposition. Paul told the Corinthians,

> *"as servants of God we commend ourselves in every way: in great endurance; in troubles, hardships and distresses; in beatings,*

> *imprisonments and riots; in hard work, sleepless nights and hunger"*   (2 Corinthians 6:4–5)

but also,

> *"in purity, understanding, patience and kindness; in the Holy Spirit and in sincere love; in truthful speech and in the power of God; with weapons of righteousness in the right hand and in the left."*   (2 Corinthians 6:6–7)

Timothy was to be diligent, too, in those areas of his life particularly specified by his spiritual father – who knew and understood him so well. Here is a case in point:

> *"Don't let anyone look down on you because you are young, but set an example for the believers in speech, in life, in love, in faith and in purity . . . **Be diligent** in these matters; give yourself wholly to them, so that everyone may see your progress. Watch your life and doctrine closely. Persevere in them, because if you do, you will save both yourself and your hearers."*
>   (1 Timothy 4:12, 15–16, my emphasis)

He is, therefore, to be:

- wary of hiding behind his youth
- careful in his conversation – *"in speech"*
- watchful of his public behavior – *"in life"*
- vigilant regarding his affections – *"in love"*
- cautious in where he placed his faith – *"in faith"*
- alert to his own appetites – *"in purity."*

All these are areas of life that, in the course of time and fellowship, are covered by wise spiritual fathering. So far as conversation and public behavior are concerned some may, I think, be inclined to dismiss them as secondary matters. The truth however, known well by fathers and mentors, is that such traits are clear indicators of our personal estimate of "the ministry," of how we see ourselves as servants of Christ. Paul saw his divine calling and vocation as the highest possible privilege, to be honored at every level of life by diligent attention to detail and duty. Look at his attitude regarding speech. It is indicated with blunt clarity in the teaching that he gave to the Ephesians:

> *"Do not let any unwholesome talk come out of your mouths, but only what is helpful for building others up according to their needs, that it may benefit those who listen."*
>
> (Ephesians 4:29)

He continues in chapter 5 in an even stronger vein. There must be no *"obscenity, foolish talk or coarse joking, which are out of place, but rather thanksgiving"* (v. 4). Why be surprised when spiritual fathers today raise the same issues? It is to be expected. They are being true to the word and spirit of the New Testament.

There arises from time to time among believers generally (usually because it has already arisen among leaders particularly) the idea that God's grace somehow delivers us from the need for careful speech, appropriate and modest appearance, and good manners. Paul's fatherly counsel to his son Timothy simply does not support this view, or the behavior that sometimes springs from it. Christian conversation, leave alone the gospel of God, is not commended by slang, vulgarity, or swearing,[3] neither is Christian ministry honored by slovenly appearance and boorish behavior, it is rather dishonored.

When thinking along these lines I find pleasure in calling to mind pastors and leaders that I know in Egypt, especially those in some of the Nile village churches. Their conversation, manners, and demeanor, usually in extremely poor circumstances, reveal the high honor and esteem in which they hold their ministry. They are a wonderful combination of cheerful generosity and pastoral dignity.

Finally Paul emphasized Timothy's need for diligence regarding personal appetites: *"Set an example . . . in purity,"* and again in 1 Timothy 5:22, *"Keep yourself pure."* In his second letter Paul tells his servant son and disciple to *"Flee the evil desires of youth . . . "* (2 Timothy 2:22). Since I will consider this further in a later chapter it is enough to say here that the temptation to sexual sin is currently rendered more acute by its promotion in the contemporary entertainment industry and by the ease with which it can be publicly and privately accessed.[4] It is also true that churches and para-church organizations may be too ready to accept as appropriate images and fashions driven by the current secular "scene."

Fathers and mentors, therefore, in talking through issues of sexual temptation and purity with sons and disciples, may find themselves thought of as somewhat out of date and reactionary. They will, I think, be willing to run the risk.

Paul's fathering, then, in all these things placed a clear emphasis on diligence, perseverance, and self-control. Both Timothy and Titus were vigorously exhorted to train and discipline themselves, to be in control of their minds, their desires, their time, and their general behavior.

> "... *train yourself to be godly. For physical training is of some value, but godliness has value for all things, holding promise for both the present life and the life to come.*" (1 Timothy 4:7–8)

They were to remember that people would be watching and following them, that the shape and content of their own lives would touch and influence the lives of other believers.

The apostle's desire was that his fathering and mentoring of Timothy and Titus would lead to their *self*-discipline, to a private strength of mind and will that would affect every part of their lives. Central to this was purity of both life and doctrine, as briefly seen already, but it also included their attitude to money and their approach to study.

Fathers and diligence with money

Paul's counsel to Timothy concerning finance was serious. Given in the context of contentment as opposed to covetousness, he states that a longing for money makes a man prey to temptation and traps him *"into many foolish and harmful desires that plunge men into ruin and destruction"* (1 Timothy 6:9). Why such stern language? Because spiritual fathers know that money, together with sex and power, are critical areas of private and personal temptation for Christian leaders. Eugene Peterson translates the passage in the following words:

> "*Lust for money brings trouble and nothing but trouble. Going down that path, some lose their footing in the faith completely and live to regret it bitterly ever after.*" (*The Message*)[5]

If a man handles money badly he must seek proper help from a discreet source – a competent friend or professional advisor – and accept counsel and assistance. A spiritual father may be involved early on but will not want to continue that involvement on a long-term basis. The son, rather than his father, must become responsible for his own affairs. A wise father will, of course, inquire from time to time whether good financial practice is in place, that debt is not mounting, and commitments are being met – and that his "son's" wife is not in the dark!

I know men who regret deeply the lack of fatherly concern and counsel over their finances during the early years of their ministry. For many their financial difficulties were due to three reasons: first, the simple fact that their financial circumstances were difficult (translation: they had very little money); second, they were expected to exercise faith and not talk about money at all; third, they were ashamed of their incompetence.

The many authentic stories of miraculous provision are testimony to God's faithfulness,[6] but it would have been a great deal better had elders and people exercised faith together with the man sent to them by God. The faith quickened by agreement generates a spiritual dynamic that has both life and abundance in it.

Spiritual fathers today are more open and likely to ask the questions that matter so far as ministry and money is concerned. This does not mean that I favor a contractual job-description approach to Christian leadership – that way of thinking, I am sure, is quite wrong.[7] Gift-ministries are sent by God to serve His kingdom interests and given by Christ to serve His church body. They are God's servants, and there is a sense, therefore, in which they cannot be "paid" for their service. What the apostle called *"this ministry"* (2 Corinthians 4:1) is an anointed administration of a divine gift and covenant: how could it possibly be evaluated? A man's various expenses should be properly met, and he may, above that, be blessed financially,[8] but his *ministry* is not a purchasable commodity: it cannot be bought – and neither can it be offered for sale.

This much, certainly, may be said: a man arrested early in his ministry by a fatherly concern regarding his handling of money, wisely mentored in a biblical approach to finance and encouraged to be self-disciplined in handling personal affairs, will have a great deal for which to be thankful in later years.

Fathers and diligence in study

"Do your best to present yourself to God as one approved, a workman who does not need to be ashamed and who correctly handles the word of truth." (2 Timothy 2:15)

Because the most significant part of our work, as said in Chapter 6, is expounding God's word, diligent application of mind to the text and meaning of Scripture is unavoidable – we will have to study. Spiritual fathers know that divine approval is bestowed upon the servant who has labored to penetrate into the meaning of His master's message until the understanding of it has passed from the page or the screen into his mind and heart. Furthermore, and blessedly, God anoints what He approves – and He approves the servant who studies and works and labors until he is handling the word of truth correctly. It is, in fact, divine approval under anointing that manifests itself in the unction and flow of the Holy Spirit upon the message. Such anointing begins with a personal determination to study; anything less will lead, eventually, to shame.

Fathers can usually tell the difference between natural charisma and divine anointing. It is possible for a while to ride the waves of natural charisma but a perceptive father, in the midst of such enthusiasm, may gently ask, "How is your study life progressing? What are you 'seeing' in Scripture? What message from God's word are you presently carrying?" He knows that the waves will subside sooner or later, that the natural assets of ready speech and an attractive manner will pall eventually if there is a lack of studied substance. Latent talents and skills are useful, but they must bow to God's word and become servants of it, not substitutes for it. Fathers, quite simply, have an ear for the message that grows up and out from the inner man, from where, through diligent study, it has been sown and watered and warmed until it has taken root. Then it is the word of life to us,[9] and passes out and into our hearers to be the word of life in them.

When our fathers listen to us in vain for that word of life, particularly over a period of time, they become restless; they know that in the long run nothing else is really going to do. Study that has reached no further than our notebooks, producing talks that run thin like watered soup from the confines of a page, fills them with concern. They are listening for something else, for a life-giving message that flows full as richest wine from the mind and heart of the inner man. The absence of such ministry will cause a spiritual father to make kindly inquiries. In a word fathers sense if we are "drinking Christ" in our reading and research (cf. John 7:37–39), if we are committed to what Richard Foster calls "the discipline of study."[10] It is out of this discipline and the filling of the Spirit that is integral to it, that the divine flow of illuminated truth proceeds.

The writer to the Hebrews made a remarkable statement about the word of God:

> *"the word of God is living and active. Sharper than any double-edged sword, it penetrates even to dividing soul and spirit, joints and marrow; it judges the thoughts and attitudes of the heart."*
>
> (Hebrews 4:12)

I suspect, however, that such penetration into those who hear it is dependent on the word penetrating the preacher first. No wonder Timothy's spiritual father and mentor charged him with the wonderful duty and privilege of sacred study,[11] for by study, if we will give ourselves to it, the Holy Spirit will penetrate and renew our minds and so, gradually, transform our lives – and that is a prerequisite for effective ministry.

"So," says the father and apostle to his son in the faith, *"keep your head in all situations, endure hardship, do the work of an evangelist, discharge all the duties of your ministry"* (2 Timothy 4:5).

Notes

1. Barney Coombs, *Apostles Today* (Sovereign World, 1996), p. 116.
2. There is an authentic and proper psychology of course, but it is either too often hidden behind a barrage of pseudo-psychology beloved of amateur counselors or submerged beneath a tide of popular but shallow jargon. The books of John White (*The Shattered Mirror*, 1987, and *Parents in Pain*, IVP, 1980, to name two) are excellent examples of a Christian psychiatrist bringing his true expertise to bear upon issues in a lucid and biblical manner.
3. This is not a denial of the need for straightforward language, in conversation or ministry. Colorful imagery and description, graphic and exciting use of words, pathos, humor, and drama, are all part of the romance and glory of preaching and teaching.
4. I understand that this kind of observation would have been true in Paul's day too (and would have been one of the reasons why he warned

Timothy to avoid *"the evil desires of youth"*). It could also be made – *was* made – about extreme "worldliness" at other times, the early eighteenth century in England, for example. Nevertheless, we are living through a period when gross sexual and social sins are being promoted as perfectly normal, and sponsored and legalized as healthy elements of a progressive and civilized society.

5. Navpress Publishing Group, 2002.

6. We have some wonderful ones of our own!

7. I came across a very fine article entitled "Ministry: Contract or Covenant?" in the broadsheet *Bread for the Journey* 1998. It was written by Derek Tidball, Principal of London Bible College, and could be read by all churches, elders, deacons, and pastors with profit. Here is a quote, "The road of the job description is the road of contract. Pastoral work should travel the road of the covenant, just as the God of all grace and the Father of our Lord Jesus Christ has done for us. To turn ministry into a contractual relationship is to betray its true nature. It is to sell our birthright for a 'mess of pottage.' Biblical language about ministry is covenant language." This is true. Ministry cannot be reduced to hourly rates, days off, the number of services to be led, visits made, sermons preached. Ministry is covenant; it interrupts annual leave, family gatherings, leisure, illness. When ministry becomes contract, ministers become professionals, or, to use the word that Jesus our covenant Shepherd used, hirelings.

8. It is also necessary that proper accounts, taxes, and payments are rendered to the government, and that any system instituted legally for this is adhered to by minister and church.

9. I do not mean by this that Scripture, at some moment of study, becomes God's word. Scripture is always God's word, in all its parts at all times, whether we can "see" it or not, whether we believe it or not. I simply mean that as we study that part of Scripture indicated and illuminated to us by the Holy Spirit it takes hold of us in a special way: it takes root in our mind and heart so that we see it with great clarity and possess it as it possesses us.

10. *Celebration of Discipline* (Hodder & Stoughton, 1999, new edn), Chapter 5.

11. So much more needs to be said about study, particularly on learning *how* to study rather than on attaining levels of knowledge. Both are important, but private study of God's word as a spiritual discipline is the source of true freedom and rest of mind and heart. If, with all our knowledge, we have not found that, we have yet to engage with true spiritual study.

Chapter 11

Fathers – and Churches

Should all those who plant or found churches be viewed as fathers? The answer, I think, is yes in a foundational sense but not necessarily so in an ongoing functional sense. All church founders and planters should be honored for their initial ministry, while some, such as the apostle Paul, are honored as both founding fathers and continuing fathers.

Other leaders, because of their ministry to a church during a particular period in its life and progress (sometimes a long period), are recognized and received as fathers in different ways. Some, because they bring to a church ministry that establishes foundations in doctrine and practice, may be perceived as apostolic fathers. This would especially be so if upon such foundations the spiritual life and worship of the church significantly deepened and developed. Others, who give guidance to churches that are passing through times of major change and spiritual renewal when a whole body of people are moving to a new level of life and function, may be thought of as prophetic fathers. Others who lead and counsel churches through periods of discord, disillusion, or hurt, would be regarded and loved as pastoral fathers.

All the gift-ministries of Ephesians 4:11 therefore – apostles, prophets, evangelists, pastors and teachers – may find themselves, at times, serving churches and leaders in a fatherly capacity, while not necessarily being fathers in a founding or planting sense. This does not mean, of course, that all gift-ministries should necessarily be thought of as spiritual fathers, or spiritual fathers inevitably thought of as gift-ministries. It is a mistake to force a father into an apostolic or pastoral jacket when it simply doesn't fit. By and large, however, those who are spiritual fathers to churches and leaders will almost certainly be gift-ministries.[1] This leaves room for a local church elder to be acknowledged and accepted over the years as a father to a church and its leaders (sometimes a succession of leaders) without having to assume an inappropriate gift-ministry label.

The elements and characteristics of fatherhood considered already in earlier chapters – representing God as head of the family and household, upholding the law of the Lord, celebrating His mighty acts and instructing his family in their meaning – combine to generally define a father as the provider, protector, and mentor of the family, with the responsibility of reproducing in his sons a desire to be the same. We should not take this to mean, however, that every element of fathering must be present in its fullness before a father can be recognized and his ministry received. Fathers grow and develop too, with the depth and value of their ministry increasing with the cultivation of character and gift.

Paul and the fathering of churches

The apostle Paul saw himself clearly as a spiritual father to churches:

> *"Even though you have ten thousand guardians in Christ, you do not have many fathers, for in Christ Jesus I became your father through the gospel."* (1 Corinthians 4:15)

He is taking pains here to show the church at Corinth the position he occupies in regard to them. Because his letter contains a severe censure of their behavior with serious warnings and instructions he is reminding them of the authority he has to address them in such a way, not the authority of an overbearing dictator but that of a loving and faithful father.

Paul has already called them children,

> *"I am not writing this to shame you, but to warn you, as my dear children."* (1 Corinthians 4:14)

His preaching of the gospel had sown the seed by which the Corinthians had been born children of God. In a sense similar to the midwife who refers to those brought to birth with her assistance as "my" children, so Paul saw himself as a father, a spiritual father, to those whom, in Christ, he had brought to new birth. He underlines the relationship by exaggerating the distinction between teachers and fathers: he is not simply one among many instructors – they have a "multitude" of those – he is their father in Christ. The warning they are to receive, therefore, is not from one of a large number of dispassionate "guardians" or teachers, but from their true spiritual father. In chapter 9 he expresses the same sentiment in another, equally entreating, manner:

> *"Are you not the result of my work in the Lord? Even though I may not be an apostle to others, surely I am to you! For you are the seal of my apostleship in the Lord."*   (1 Corinthians 9:1–2)

It is quite clear, therefore, that Paul saw himself as an apostolic father to the church in Corinth and was reminding them of the fact in preparation for the content and tone of what was to come in his letter.

He goes on in the same passage to encourage them, as his children, to imitate him and, as an example of what he means, sends Timothy, *"my son whom I love, who is faithful in the Lord"* (1 Corinthians 4:16), to support them in this. Paul does not send one of those many teachers, Peter or Apollos, for example – their presence, given the sectarian spirit of the Corinthians at the time, would have inflamed the situation. He sends instead a spiritual son, hoping that they will see in him the kind of attitude that spiritual children should adopt toward their fathers.

Paul holds the same spiritual father relationship to the Galatian churches. This is plain from the words already considered in Galatians 4:19,

> *"My dear children, for whom I am again in the pains of childbirth until Christ is formed in you ..."*

In this troubled appeal Paul describes himself as being *"again in the pains of childbirth,"* a phrase that reveals the high level of spiritual responsibility he felt toward them.

To the Thessalonian church Paul is, again, their spiritual father. However, his approach to them, and the language he employs, is quite different. There is no disappointment or reproach here, only expressions of pleasure and affirmation; he says,

> *"For you know that we dealt with each of you as a father deals*
> *with his own children, encouraging, comforting and urging you to*
> *live lives worthy of God, who calls you into his kingdom and*
> *glory."*   (1 Thessalonians 2:11–12)

Paul was as ready to encourage and comfort his Thessalonian children as to reprimand and warn those in Corinth and Galatia. We should note his even-handedness. Fathers cannot afford to develop a kind of trouble-shooting mentality where encounters and conversations simply become occasions for constantly confronting problems and working through difficulties. There is so much to encourage and affirm, so much for which to be thankful. Even with the Corinthians Paul seasoned his reproach with affirmations of their rich ministry and spiritual gifts (1 Corinthians 1:4–7).

Finding fathers

In Paul's case, therefore, the fathering of churches was rooted in his original preaching, planting, and teaching ministry. He evangelized towns and cities in Galatia on his first mission journey (Acts 13 – 14), and did the same in the major trade route centers of Philippi, Thessalonica, Corinth and Ephesus[2] on his second (Acts 17:1–15; 18:1–22). His subsequent ministry to them, particularly in his epistles, was given, as we have seen, on the basis of the spiritual father–child relationship in which they were joined together, a framework fundamental to his apostolic fatherhood.

Among long-established churches, however, connecting with fathers is necessarily different. There would have to be a recognition and acceptance of those who, by character and ministry, prove themselves to be true fathers and mentors. The leaders of a church may invite such a person to spend time with them in fellowship and ministry, and discover in the process that they have made a "divine connection" with a gift-ministry who becomes a father to them and the church.

Or, again, a church, though blessed with apostolic, prophetic or pastoral gifts, may still find itself in circumstances that call for fatherly wisdom and prudence. Leaders already serving in the church may not be able to help in a particular instance, for various reasons,[3] but will happily recommend and receive a proven spiritual father.

Personal reflection

I have been unexpectedly blessed in this way over recent years. Had I been told early on in my ministry that some would later view me as a spiritual father I would have smiled in disbelief. It has become nevertheless a delightful privilege to serve a small number of leaders and churches at home and abroad in this way.

In one instance it began like this: I was speaking at Spring Harvest in 1994 when a young man, at the close of a session on local church leadership, waited to speak with me. He introduced himself as an elder of a church on the south coast and asked, with some diffidence, if I would consider visiting and spending some time with him. He wrote to me later and put the request in writing. I felt, after a while, that it would be appropriate to meet with him at his home. That meeting marked the beginning of a long and happy relationship with the church and its leaders.[4]

By far the most usual way, therefore, for churches and spiritual fathers to find one another is through a bond that develops between a church leader and a father-figure, where mutual recognition of the Holy Spirit's leading forms a basis for an ongoing relationship. Such a relationship may remain personal but this would be unusual. Normally it would be recognized by the leader's colleagues or team if he has one, and eventually by the church itself.

Fathers, teams, and churches

I want to look further at fathers and churches but, in order to do so, will have to say something, at this point, about leaders and teams.

Two things in this respect seem to me to be elemental: first, the need to understand the divine calling and sending of servant-leaders and their carrying by delegation a deposit of spiritual authority, and, second, the use made of that authority by such leaders to delegate responsibility to others in a framework of servanthood, discipleship, and accountability.

The receiving of divinely called, sent, and authorized servant-leaders is central to the restoring of God's kingdom on earth.[5] A kingdom is established where the authority of the King's will and word is acknowledged and obeyed.[6] This is the way with all kingdoms, and supremely with the kingdom of God. In a true servant sent by God the will and word of God is paramount. By the submission and obedience of such a servant, therefore, His kingdom is established in them and its authority manifested through them – for only those under authority have authority.

Christ – perfectly adjusted to the law of the ages

The supreme "model" of this called and sent servant-leadership is the Father's Son. In the Lord Jesus Christ there was a manifestation of the life of the kingdom of God in His own life through submission to His Father's will and obedience to His Father's word. The sovereign authority of His Father, therefore, was manifested in His living and expounded in His teaching. Submission and obedience were the moral dynamic of His leadership, the personal and historic embodiment of the kingdom of God.

There was, therefore, through Christ's submissive obedience to His Father's will and word, a release on earth of the law of the Lord, of the essential energy and sovereign authority by which all things exist, consist, and cohere, that is, of the kingdom of God.[7] This is why, when Jesus spoke the word of the Father, the life and authority by which the entire universe holds together[8] was in His words – *"No-one ever spoke the way this man does"* (John 7:46). And Jesus Himself said,

> *"The Spirit gives life; the flesh counts for nothing. The words I have spoken to you are spirit and they are life."*   (John 6:63)

His announcement in the synagogue at Nazareth that the prophecy of Isaiah (Isaiah 61:1–2) was being fulfilled in Him at that moment was startling in the extreme; *"Today,"* said Jesus, *"this scripture is fulfilled in your hearing"* (Luke 4:21). The stupendous moment for the inauguration of the manifestation on earth of God's kingdom authority – an authority by which good news for the poor, freedom for prisoners, recovery of sight for the blind, release for the oppressed, and the year of the Lord's favor, would be proclaimed – had arrived. With such personal conviction and public boldness came Jesus, preaching and teaching the good news of the kingdom. Historically and spiritually the rule of God had broken through.

How did such a stupendous breakthrough happen? It happened because in every aspect of His being and nature, in thought, word, and deed, the Lord Jesus Christ was perfectly adjusted to the divine law of the ages. He was the *"Servant of the Lord"* supreme (Isaiah 42:1; 52:13; 53:11), the One "sent" by the Father (John 20:21).[9] Jesus Himself said,

> *"My food is to do the will of Him who **sent** me and to finish **His** work."* (John 4:34, my emphasis)

How clear this is. Christ was personally sent as the Lord's Servant-leader. His Father's sovereign will and rule was released in Him and through Him so that the kingdom of heaven was in all He thought and said and did, it was "in Him," therefore, it was "here." The powers of the age to come had broken through into this present age in the life and ministry of the chosen and sent One, the servant King.

Disciples to be with Him

When Christ chose and called His disciples to be *"with Him"* (Mark 3:14) it was to reproduce in them through discipleship the same kingdom principles by which He Himself manifested the rule of God, and so bring into being a "team" of servants who would "live" the kingdom together.

This is how the kingdom comes and grows, by submission to the will, and obedience to the word, of spiritual authority, a supernatural process that takes place by reproductive discipleship rather than managerial strategy. Biblical "team ministry," therefore, comes about by recognition of spiritual authority in a called and sent servant-leader. God's kingdom advances through the team he chooses, and those they serve, as submission and obedience to authority becomes a life principle in their covenant relationship.

There remained, nevertheless, no doubt as to where the spiritual authority lay. Jesus said,

> *"You call me 'Teacher' and 'Lord,' and rightly so, for that is what I am. Now that I, your Lord and Teacher, have washed your feet, you also should wash one another's feet."* (John 13:13–14)

Recognition, and acceptance, of spiritual authority (*"Unless I wash you, you have no part with me,"* John 13:8) makes possible the process of discipleship by which we may properly express the kingdom of God – in willing submission to service (*"not just my feet but my hands and my head as well!"* John 13:9) and the joyful submission of service to authority.

Looking, with these principles in mind, at the contemporary emphasis on leadership teams will bring us, I believe, to this conclusion: that the accent on the called and anointed "servant of the Lord," the "man sent by God" to speak His word and lead His people, is less prominent today than it is in Scripture and in the subsequent scope of church history.

As we have seen, such servant-leaders make disciples, delegate responsibility, and share ministry. It is difficult, however, to see the management structure of much modern team thinking (particularly if equal responsibility or collegiality is the modus operandi) functioning upon this basis of submission to delegated spiritual authority. It cannot therefore, I think, be viewed as the biblical norm.

To be sure, gift-ministries *are* given to work together in covenant relationship and team.[10] Paul chose disciples and fellow-workers to travel and serve with him in this way. Some of them became long-time friends and ministry colleagues, but it is difficult to read back into such apostolic relationships the modern team concept of equal and shared responsibility which, I suspect, is an overreaction to what has been described as "one-man-band" or "lone ranger" ministry.

There is need for a recovery of emphasis on servant-leaders called and sent by God with spiritual authority, and for a spirit of servanthood, humility, accountability, and submission to flourish among such leaders and those chosen and appointed by them – for this is the way God's kingdom comes and grows.

When fathers meet with teams

Having looked at some principles basic to spiritual leadership, team, and the manifestation of the kingdom of God, we may now be better able to consider fathers and mentors in their ministry to churches and teams.

I have noted that apostolic fathers, when coming alongside a team or church, look almost immediately for the line of spiritual authority. They know how fundamental this is to the church fulfilling its kingdom and gospel mandate. Their understanding of the dynamics of spiritual authority means that, in the main, fathers view leaders and teams theologically and spiritually rather than managerially and strategically. These categories are not entirely exclusive of each other, of course, for good management and strategy can be spiritual. What matters here is the foundation and priority, and that lies clearly with the calling and authority of Christ Himself and its reproductive "succession" in those called by Him, those who are filled with His word and His Spirit in order to make disciples by the same spiritual authority. When spiritual fathers meet with leaders, teams and congregations, therefore, their understanding of calling and authority is central to their ministry of *"strengthening the churches"* (Acts 15:41).

For example, a leader may be troubled with doubts about his call and be struggling to make good his spiritual authority. If this becomes crucial he may lose his way. His team and the church will languish in the shadow of his fears. How do spiritual fathers serve in such circumstances? Advise better man management? Help the leader and team devise a vision statement? Bring in a purpose and planning consultancy? All these may have some relevance, but none of them, together, singly, or with a host of other "remedies" will make any lasting difference if the call of God in the man of God, and the spiritual authority that goes with it, is doubted, neglected, lost, or missing. A wise father will attend to this as priority because he knows that it is the very foundation and framework of servant-leadership. It will take time. Reasons for doubt or neglect often lie hidden and problems invariably arise that appear to have little or no connection at all with the loss of confidence. A father will gently take the leader, his family, the team, and the church to his heart as he listens, prays, talks, and supports them by his presence, wisdom, and care. And all the while he is believing for the spark of faith that will hear the call again. It is for the call that he is looking and working – because he knows there is no alternative. And his heart will rejoice when he sees it.

As a father meets in fellowship with a leader and his team he slowly gets to know them. He observes their style and manner, and in time becomes conscious of the unspoken interplay between their various personalities and temperaments. He notes the man with the quick mind alongside those who are more cautious and deliberate. He sees (and hears) the articulate man who is never lost for words, and his friend who is slow to speak. He marks those who see an issue and its outcome quickly, and those again who take time to look at each and every angle of a matter.

The true father knows that the careful words of a quiet thinker can help to move forward the excited zeal of those who have already seen the destination but have no idea whatsoever on how to actually get there. He knows, too, that some on the team will still be giving a "divine idea" mature consideration in a year's time with the activists suspended in agonized frustration by the endless talk. He sees all this and more, and, by observation, question, comment and encouragement may, without imposition, assist decision and progress. He will make observations that bring balance to discussions, raise questions that seem not to have been thought of, and consequences that are not being sufficiently considered.

A father will often help a team to identify the crux of a matter, something not always easy with a close-knit group of friends. With his wider eye he is able to distinguish those who are penetrating to the heart of an issue, and encourage them to speak. In this instance he does two things: he avoids taking control and he encourages those on the team who have insight. He is adept, too, in seeing a problem that is being quietly ignored by the team in the hope that it will go away. If he senses that in fact it needs to be handled or talked through he may, for a while, take a lead and guide the discussion.

When sharing in fellowship with a team a father sees those things that would be better left; he knows that not everything has to be handled there and then. He sees the team leader's momentary frustration, the man slightly offended, the rebuke that is too sharp. He will talk through some of these things with the leader at a later date: "You could have listened a little more to Tom, I know he's slower than Mike, but he does get to the root of an issue;" "Why did you cut George short? It was too sharp;" "There's a problem with Will, do you know what it is?" "You handled Simon and Tony really well. Do you know why they spark?" "Your quietness on that particular issue was good, I thought for a moment you were going to react."

Fathers see the good things too: the desire for God's glory and honor, the evident affection that team members have for each other, the ringing note of faith, the willingness to submit to Scripture or a prophetic word. He will wisely affirm these things: "Your passion for God's glory is more valuable than you know"; "You have a real sense of affection – appreciate and keep it"; "There is a rising tide of faith among you – pray it through, identify its purpose, seize the moment."

The team that will not work

Some leaders inherit members from previous teams and wonder, sometimes, what on earth they are going to do with them. Others find themselves with no team at all and are unsure how to go about forming one. I sometimes visit churches to find teams that have evolved on their own by a kind of "natural selection" with no called leader at all – and often with unique and interesting ideas about their roles and responsibilities.

And then there is the team that quite simply will not work.

Many spiritual fathers, in their time, will have faced this problem themselves. They will have felt their own inadequacy, shed their own tears, and called upon their own apostles, fathers, and mentors. As a result they have few illusions about team. They know too that, because covenant relationships and responsibility are fundamental to the church's mandate to preach the gospel of the kingdom and of the Lord Jesus Christ, leaders and teams are a target for enemy action.

Because of these things a father often comes to a team in difficulty from a perspective other than, "We *must* make this work because team is the only way to do leadership." He knows that to push such a dogma to its limits usually adds to the tension and may increase the heartache.

Some leaders, faced with a team that is not working, will gather up their energies into much time and effort, lay stress on the doctrines and principles to be understood, and seek to instill into team members the attitude and behavior required. Others will resort to extended prayer times or "spiritual warfare," while others will initiate sessions of "open-heart surgery" in an attempt to create vulnerability and so discover one mind and one voice.

But an experienced father knows that with the best will in the world some teams are simply not going to work. Relationships that once were good can become uncomfortable – and nice men will disagree. Different temperaments cannot be forced to be other than what they are, and any attempt to compel "unity" is a contradiction of the reality.

Of course it can be more serious: "His wife controls him;" "He's become attached to another leader," "He criticizes the team;" "He bullies his family." In these instances fathers will advise personal confrontation, then, if that is not successful, they will advocate the biblical procedure of making a further approach with one or two other leaders. Nevertheless, after such loving fellowship or clear confrontation (sometimes over a long period), the leader may have to accept fatherly insight and judgment: "I'm sorry, but really, it isn't going to work. You can't force him and you can't make it happen. You will have to let go and take a fresh look at the relationships and understanding that you still have."

A word of caution. Not all team trouble has in it the seeds of disintegration. Fathers have learned that relationships can be strained, often as a result of small things – "He didn't visit me when I was down;" "He went quiet on us;" "He's always late;" "Communication on this team is abysmal" – and will be more relaxed about them. An exasperated leader will often see these things in crisis terms to be dealt with by stern and drastic measures, whereas a spiritual father may simply see tired, misplaced, harassed or frustrated men and suggest some loving personal fellowship to talk things through – and sometimes to loosen things up.

Paul had "team problems." At one time he refused to work with the young John Mark and had a serious argument with Barnabas because of it. They had, in fact, *"such a sharp disagreement that they parted company"* (see Acts 15:37–41). When you consider that it was Barnabas who initially sought Paul out and brought him into fellowship with the Christian community, commending his conversion and ministry to the apostles and elders, the breakdown between them was sad indeed. On another occasion Paul fell out seriously with Peter regarding doctrine and behavior and *"opposed him to his face"* in public (see Galatians 2:11–15). Instead, however, of spending endless hours trying to make these relationships work in order to fulfill some kind of team ideal, the dominating concern of their lives triumphed – they continued to spread the gospel of the kingdom of God and of the Lord Jesus Christ and to encourage and strengthen the churches.

One final word

Fellowship within a leadership team does not always carry fathering on into the church itself. There could be a number of reasons for this. The team may not be relating well to the church. It is quite possible for a team to develop a life of its own apart from the people. It may create its own means of blessing with conferences, retreats, leadership functions, and events. It may be taken up with its own problems and its own blessings. It may actually become more attached to a movement or to a network than it is to the local church – which may have become a nuisance and a hindrance to the blessing of the team! A team can forget that it exists, not for itself, but for God, for His kingdom and His people.

A wise father will quickly see when a team has become an end in itself, and will insist on challenging it. He will remind them that the Lord Jesus Christ sent His disciples to serve and work among the people. He may highlight the risen Lord's discussion with the chastened and forgiven Peter regarding his, Peter's, future ministry: *"Simon son of John, do you truly love me **more than these?**"* (John 21:15, my emphasis). "These," I think, were Peter's friends and their old fishing relationships. Peter insisted that he did love the Lord more than them all, but it is Christ's reply to Peter that should be noted. Peter's insistent confession of love was met with the divine direction, "feed and care for my flock, both lambs and sheep." They were to be love's priority. Team must never take the place of church. Our Lord Jesus Christ discipled the twelve for this purpose, that they should go and make disciples in their turn.

> *"It was he who gave some to be apostles, some to be prophets, some to be evangelists, and some to be pastors and teachers, **to prepare God's people for works of service, so that the body of Christ may be built up** until we all reach unity in the faith and in the knowledge of the Son of God and become mature, attaining to the whole measure of the fullness of Christ."*
> (Ephesians 4:11–13, my emphasis)

In 1930, in a small but influential book among the Assembly of God churches in the UK, Donald Gee, with apostolic insight, wrote the following:

> "It is spiritual fathers that the Assemblies need so much, and sadly lack in many places. Something more is required than 'leaders'; something more than 'preachers'; something more than nominal figure-heads: every flock of God needs fathering. A vital element is lacking where there is not a personal caring for individual souls, and an interest in them that is prepared to go to the point of sacrifice if the need arise."[11]

Two things gladden my heart as the chill mists of ever more management slowly rise around us: one, that history is replete with accounts of those who have heard the trumpet, burnt their bridges, refused to be put down, taken up their cross, and spread the gospel of God and His grace in places where committees said it could not be done; and, two, that there is a new generation of apostolic adventurers, full of passion for God, filled with His word and His Spirit, who will not be ensnared by the sophisticated trappings of natural technique and growth formulae, designed eventually to strangle calling and prophetic vision. Theological, worshipful, radical, godly, they are rising to dispel the fog of worldliness and "spiritual" entertainment, religious quackery, and libertarian anti-biblical dogma. This is another day. Their day.

> "Quit you like men, be strong, wax valiant in the fight,
> See! yonder Captain leads the throng, in Whom is
> 　　　your delight."[12]

Old fashioned words? Maybe, but maybe not. They are part of the divine continuum. The language breathes a former time, the truth is timeless.

Notes

1. The list-label-catalogue mode of so much western thought is often imposed upon Scripture to the detriment of function. The flow-chart mentality tends to confine us to boxes and allows little room for "overlapping." Michael Eaton, suggesting that pastors and teachers are a "composite" gift-ministry, says, "I think it better to think of two ministries that are closely related. Pastors are teachers who are good with

people, teachers are pastors who are good at exposition" (*Preaching Through the Bible – Ephesians* (Sovereign World International), p. 74.

2. Paul revisited Ephesus on his third mission journey for a longer period (Acts 19). The account of his work and ministry there is full of faith, preaching and teaching, signs, many converts, great excitement, and danger!

3. There may be a personal or family connection with a particular issue that makes it inappropriate for a leader to be involved, or a theological position may make objective discussion difficult, or again, too great an emotional involvement may render dispassionate contribution impossible.

4. Nick May has always maintained that God prompted him to approach me (I was entirely unknown to him at the time) and, of course, that prompting must be recognized as a significant element in the ensuing relationship.

5. This is not to say that God's kingdom has ever been absent from the earth. How could it be? It is never absent from anywhere for all that exists has its being as a result of, and within, His sovereign decree, dominion, and government: *"The Lord has established his throne in heaven, and his kingdom rules over all"* (Psalm 103:19). No, the kingdom of God is the realm of His will and rule, the whole of creation, even where it is fallen, lies, because of, and for the sake of its existence, necessarily within that rule. We are therefore in and under God's kingdom rule, even as sinners, but the life of the kingdom rule is not in us. Though His glorious kingdom be all around us and we live in it and because of it, we cannot see it, until, that is, we are born again. It is the life of God's kingdom rule in and among fallen men that is being restored, and that had its inauguration in the coming, living, dying and rising of the Father's beloved Son and Servant, our Lord Jesus Christ.

6. *"Your kingdom come, your will be done, on earth as it is in heaven . . . "* (Matthew 6:7).

7. This is why Christ's coming brought a sword (Matthew 10:34), because the law of the Lord, the authority of God's kingdom in Christ, was an immediate challenge to the present world system enslaved and controlled by sin, for *"sin is lawlessness"* (1 John 3:4). Conflict was therefore inevitable, and still is, though consummation of the kingdom is gloriously assured as a result of Christ's redeeming death and resurrection. Even now God's kingdom rule is advancing in those who, through repentance and faith in Christ, are *"rescued . . . from the dominion of darkness and brought . . . into the kingdom of the Son he loves"* (Colossians 1:13).

8. Colossians 1:17.

9. Christ is said to be "sent" by the Father at least thirty times in the Gospel of John.

10. I have worked in partnership for nineteen years with my friend and colleague Andrew Parfitt in Maidstone, England, and with teams of elders that we have appointed to serve churches.

11. *Concerning Shepherds and Sheepfolds* (Assemblies of God Publishing House, 1930), p. 10.

12. Ernest T. Mellor, *Redemption Hymnal* (1960 ed.), No. 428.

Chapter 12

Receiving a Father's Ministry

A proud spirit needs, but cannot always "hear," a father's voice. A submissive spirit will be able to both hear it and appreciate it. The apostle Paul said,

> *"I **kneel** before the Father from whom his whole family in heaven and on earth derives its name."*
>
> (Ephesians 3:14–15, my emphasis)

Kneeling symbolizes a deference and respect that does not sit easily with self-assertion and aggressive individualism. If we are self-satisfied and self-assured we may even disparage those who look for the care and concern of a father, thinking them weak. This is a mistake. All men, including strong men, need at times the caring arm of a loving father around their shoulders, and the listening ear of a wise mentor for their support.

Because a man appears strong it does not follow that he is omni-competent and able to handle anything. Capable men feel things deeply, will sometimes weep like children, and long, while surrounded by many admirers, for the personal care of a father. To confuse such humility with weakness is a shallow misjudgment. In those who are truly strong there is a meekness that sits, childlike, at the feet of others. It is not the great who lack the "weakness" to be fathered, their humility is integral to their greatness: it is the irresolute man who, believing himself strong reveals his obstinate frailty in disdain of brokenness – and in faint praise of fathers. Humility, in our present way of thinking, rubs a diffident shoulder with the high profile world of self-assurance and hype, and quietly withdraws. If we are to benefit significantly from the ministry of fathers and mentors we will have to bring humility out of retirement.

The divine continuum

It is the submissive spirit, the spirit of humility, that causes young men in a rising move of God to bow their heads under the ministering hands of fathers from a previous day. So the classic Pentecostal prophet and teacher Howard Carter (1891–1971) blessed the young Terry Virgo and Sandy Millar, and the Pentecostal apostle and pioneer Willy Burton (1886–1971) touched the life of Roger Forster and inspired the ministry of Barney Coombs.[1] How many leaders in the charismatic renewal in England in the latter half of the twentieth century made their way to the Bournemouth flat of Harold Horton (1881–1970)[2] to receive the gift of the Spirit we simply do not know. It is a fact, however, that the divine continuum of the Spirit passes from fathers to sons irrespective of denomination and education. It flows like a river through the pioneers of one generation to the pilgrims of the next. It flows through minds deep and old with understanding and wisdom to minds young with passion and zeal, from the fathers who dream to the sons who see visions, from the mothers in Israel to the daughters of promise, from hands old with the grace of yesterday to hearts filled with faith for tomorrow. It is the river that flows from age to age, from the Father and the Son through the fathers to the sons so that one generation shall praise the Lord to another and tell of His wonders. It flows on through councils and creeds, sustains faith in dark ages and doubt, refreshes reform and revival, carries its sons to the ends of the earth to become fathers in their turn, gathers up the rag ends of existential disintegration and postmodern despair, and breaks out in the back streets of a thousand cities to confound darkness and death with the Father's everlasting love and the Son's endless obedience and resurrection life.

Being open to honesty and admonition

We will need a submissive spirit because a true father will not shrink from speaking honestly to us. Learning to receive admonition is part of a God-ordained process for our adjustment and development. Close friends may love us too much to tell us the truth.

Speaking the truth to spiritual children, however, is not always easy. We live in a user-friendly, affirm-me culture where honest counsel is too often viewed as discouragement and the cult of the positive looks sideways at straightforward rebuke. It is, as R.T. Kendal so often says, "always right to be gracious." There is no justification for being unkind, but there is need for honest appraisal and plain speaking, and fathers are apt to be the ones to do it. Paul was certainly into honest appraisal in his fatherly concern for the Corinthians:

> *"In the following directives I have no praise for you for your meetings do more harm than good."* (1 Corinthians 11:17)

He says this in the midst of much stern rebuke. In his second letter to them he writes:

> *"We have spoken freely to you, Corinthians, and opened wide our hearts to you. We are not withholding our affection from you, but you are withholding yours from us. As a fair exchange – **I speak as to my children** – open wide your hearts also."*
> (2 Corinthians 6:11–13, my emphasis)

Here are faithful and strong words from a true father. How would we feel about this kind of rebuke today? He speaks of causing them sorrow, but rejoices that it led them to repent (2 Corinthians 7:8–9), and ends the letter by excusing his severity on the grounds that it would mean his not being *"harsh in the use of authority"* when he eventually visited them (2 Corinthians 13:10).

Paul spoke of his license to deal with them in this way as *"the authority the Lord gave me for building you up, not tearing you down,"* and that is the whole point. Paul knew that true fathering involves a dual responsibility: one, to face issues and speak honestly in order to build sons, and two, to encourage faith and speak gracefully in order to bless sons. All building and no blessing will make us too hard,[3] all blessing and no building will make us too soft. I suspect that the pendulum is swinging, at present, a little too far in the "blessing" direction.

I would have to say that some of those fathers who gave me

time and loved me best were often brusque, with a peculiar skill in frankness. A young ministry assistant, I sat discomfited in one council meeting as an older minister said, "I received the letter too late, Mr Chairman. Our brother Newberry is dilatory, I have told him so. We hope he will improve." Yet I knew true affection and care from that spiritual father.

The answer, if we have become too soft under a surfeit of "blessing," is certainly not an excessive swing in the other direction, but a restoring of the balance between the two – and fathers are especially good at balance.

But not all sons are amenable to a father's ministry.

Sons who fail to benefit from a father's ministry

▶ **Some "sons" are simply willful**. They believe, always, that they are right. It is an arrogance that robs them of the ear to hear and a willingness to learn. Moreover, such sons often cannot see that this is what they are like. We should not, with this in mind, immediately think of the loud young man with the brash manner. That is not always an indication of willfulness. Some quiet and gentle people are as stubborn as mules and arrogant with it. They will often smile quietly, look saintly, and hear nothing.

Over a number years I gave a great deal of time to a young couple who were amiable, gentle, and so far as I could see filled with desire for God. We spent many evenings in conversation together. It took me too long, however, to realize that in fact they were not listening to me at all. They had no ear for my heart and no love for my voice; they were not, in truth, "my sheep." They took my time for their own ends and, when I would not serve those ends, walked quietly but deliberately away. It was willful obstinacy dressed in a quiet coat.

▶ **Some "sons" are looking for their own advice**. They have made up their minds and simply want their own decisions confirmed. To be able to quote an authority, a father, who agrees with them strengthens their hand, particularly if they are serving with elders or leaders who refuse to be pushed or rushed. They will "use" a father of some reputation to force an issue. Fathers usually know quickly when this is happening. They know, too, when they are being canvassed on an issue, when they are expected to come up with the "right" answer or affirm a course of action. A true father will not be used in this way. "I know what you want," he may say, "but I'm afraid I can't agree. You are making a mistake and should think again. This is not the way to go."

▶ **Some "sons" use a father for their own ends**. They ask for time and guidance but rarely take it. This is often because the notion of a spiritual father appeals to them rather than the reality of his ministry. It is being able to say, "I have a relationship with such and such a man; he fathers me, he is my mentor," that is important. In this case it is not the ministry of the father that is valued but the reflected light of his reputation and connection. Any relationship with the father is secondary; his care and time is undervalued and his counsel rarely received.

▶ **Some "sons" are not prepared to be accountable**. Fathers will look for an account after a course of action has been decided upon: "We spent some time talking through that issue and agreed together on the way forward, how has it gone?" When the answer wanders its way around a number of excuses for lack of progress there is a problem. When this happens on a regular basis it becomes clear that the real difficulty is an aversion to following an agreed procedure: there is no sense of accountability.

Fathering, as already seen, is much more than simply telling sons what to do. This we know. But the fact remains that where no account is rendered regarding those things that *are* discussed and agreed on, mentoring becomes difficult.

Expectations – in what will a spiritual father be interested?

We must not be surprised at a father's interest in many different things, we must expect it. In conversation he will often take us far and wide before "homing in." He knows that our guard will be up if he simply keeps to the "spiritual" track. And anyway, a true father will be interested in all the ideas and views we have.

When Cyril Bridgeland invited me to his home for "fellowship" he opened up the most fascinating discussion on a wide variety of things – hobbies, books, holidays, children, photography, do it yourself, cooking, and the detective stories of Earle Stanley Gardner – and then without the blink of an eyelid, "Do you *really* love God?" He was genuinely interested in all the other things and talked about them freely with understanding and fun – until my guard was down. Then his questions were searching and penetrating. He cheerfully challenged me, saying with a chuckle, "I want to know what makes you tick."

Here are some of the things that you will inevitably find a father and mentor talking about with you.

► **What you do in your "spare" time**. As A.W. Tozer says, the true direction of our lives is revealed by what our minds turn to when we have nothing else to think about. Fathers may appear intrusive when they talk with us at this level. The truth is they know that what occupies the mind is a source from which ministry flows, the major source. Ultimately we minister what we are. We must study and we must pray, but what comes through in the end is the life that we love. If our mind and heart is set upon that life, that nature, then God's people will be fed and Christ's body nourished.

► **The books you are reading**. Not just the "holy" ones, but the magazines, newspapers, fiction and novels that also occupy our shelves.[4] Fathers know that leaders and pastors must be in touch with their times, that while inextricably connected with the life and ministry of the historic Church, we are for today and tomorrow. They will, however, encourage us to read contemporary theological and spiritual literature too: Martyn Lloyd-Jones, Wayne Grudem, John Stott, John Piper, Alister McGrath, J.I. Packer, Richard Foster. On the other hand I never knew a father yet who did not insist on the reading of some spiritual classics.[5]

► **How you do things**. My father said to me again and again, "If you are going to do it, son, do it properly." What a great maxim for seeking and serving God and His kingdom. Do we have a desire for excellence in ministry, excellence in character and content as well as in presentation? Do we ensure that things are done well? True fathers are never happy with the half-hearted, the shabby, or the mediocre.

▶ **Whom you are "playing" with**. All fathers are careful about those with whom their children play. You can hear the concern in a parent's voice – "I don't want to find you playing with them any more," or "Don't spend your time with him, he'll not do you any good." There will be times when your spiritual father will say quite plainly, "It would be better if you saw less of him, the relationship is not helpful," and the frustration will be that you simply cannot see why. And what is even more annoying, your father cannot or will not give a reason for his counsel. Sometimes the sheer attractiveness of certain people shines in our eyes so that we cannot see serious defects, particularly lack of personal discipline. If you "play" with an undisciplined friend for too long you will be affected yourself by his problem – but by then you'll not be able to see it.

On the perimeter of the church in Maidstone a man of winning disposition and novel insights made a practice of attaching himself to young believers. He himself would never make any form of commitment to the church body, but would talk encouragingly of a leader's ministry from time to time if it ran in line with his own ideas. He was a menace because he appeared both spiritual and radical. A number of good people over the years, especially young men and couples, were spoiled by him. Elders and fathers in the church were wise to his tactics but found it difficult to warn against him effectively; people were unwilling to accept counsel along the lines of "don't play with him" – and detailing his shortcomings only made it worse. This is why fathers will warn us of certain people, but not always give details.

▶ **Your personal desires and ambitions**. A father will often ask, "What is in your heart? What do you really want? What do you see? What is your overwhelming desire?" He knows that lack of desire leads to loss of direction. If you don't know what you want, you won't know what to do. And there is little that will touch a father with heartache so much as a lack of desire for life in his son. To sense the loss of dreams, to see the fire burn low, to be chilled by the sight of dying embers, this is sadness indeed.

Sons burning with devotion and desire will share their hearts with fathers and mentors – "I want to be like this, I want a church like this, I want to understand this." How does a father respond to such expressions? I can only say that it will gladden his heart and light his eyes with pleasure. He knows that no amount of learning, information, or personality can take the place of desire, devotion and zeal. To hear passion in the voice of a son will be music to his ears.

Notes

1. All influential leaders on the British Church scene: Terry Virgo is a founding apostle and senior leader of New Frontier; Sandy Millar is vicar of Holy Trinity, Brompton, which has developed the Alpha Course; Roger Forster is the founding apostle of Ichthus Christian Fellowship, a theologian and expositor; Barney Coombs, as already mentioned, is a senior apostle among the Salt and Light churches, and pastors in Vancouver, Canada.
2. Harold Horton put the apostolic teaching of Howard Carter into his book *The Gifts of the Spirit* in 1934. It was a "pioneer book" and passed through seven editions. In 1982 it was published in Dutch, French, and German.
3. That's if we survive!
4. This must also include, I think, the videos, cassettes, CDs and Internet sites to which we turn.
5. I am often astonished, and concerned, at young leaders who appear to be happily ignorant of Thomas à Kempis' *Imitation of Christ*, Bunyan's *Pilgrim's Progress*, Calvin's *Institutes*, A.A. Hodge's *Outlines of Theology*, Spurgeon's *Metropolitan Tabernacle Pulpit*, and Tozer's *Knowledge of the Holy*.

Chapter 13

Fathers – and Passion

It is possible that the word "father," because of its association with experience and maturity, may create in our minds a rather slow, benign, and dispassionate image. It is certainly true that wisdom walks with a measured tread and the best counsel comes with settled and careful consideration. It is true, too, that speed is not necessarily spiritual. But none of this should be taken to mean that spiritual fathers lack passion and fire. Nothing could be further from the truth. Looking at many older leaders I am astounded at their enthusiasm, work rate, and sheer zest for living.

When Donald and Eunice Crook – fifty packed years of fervent gospel ministry in India and South Africa – came home to Maidstone to "retire" among our churches at seventy-five and seventy-eight respectively, their continued enthusiasm, vivacity, visiting, preaching, and enjoyment of life simply left many younger people standing bemused in their wake.

Norman Young, pastor and leader of the Walthamstow Assembly of God in North-east London for so many years, was a remarkable man. He was one of four brothers converted and called by God through the apostolic ministry of Stephen Jeffries in Bishop Auckland in 1927. My wife came to Christ under Mr Young's ministry in London and talks of him still. He was her father in Christ, authoritative ("Remove that make up young lady, Christ cannot be seen through it; and cover up your arms and legs"), zealous (most of his preaching, even his teaching, ended up as a gospel message with an appeal), and passionately Pentecostal. "You must be baptized in the Spirit, young lady. It is necessary in order to live your Christian life. Come into the vestry." Together with Mr Howes, the church elder, Mr Young laid hands on Pat, prayed for her, and she was immediately immersed in the Spirit. New tongues poured from her lips in praise to God as the initial evidence of a fullness that, so far as I am aware, has never diminished. No matter how such "despotic" pastoring might be viewed today (can I hear "legalistic dictator" being muttered somewhere?), Mr Young (he was rarely called anything else) was one of a company of classic Pentecostal leaders whose like we shall not see again. They were sons of the pioneers and fathers to a generation.[1] When I think of them I cannot help feeling that something has been lost.

Norman Young was an unusual mentor. While I was a student at the Assembly of God Bible School at Kenley[2] he asked me to preach one Sunday evening at the Walthamstow church. I did so but made the mistake of being humorous during my ministry. There was much laughter, but not from Mr Young. "Come into the vestry,"[3] he said afterwards. I was roundly chastised for indulging myself at the expense of the gospel. As you can see I have not forgotten it after nearly forty years, though I am still sometimes humorous.

John Nelson Parr, the remarkable pastor-evangelist of Bethshan Tabernacle, Manchester, during the years of the mid twentieth century, was a father in Christ to hundreds of believers and a spiritual mentor to dozens of church leaders. With a gruff air and a grave voice he would often ask – usually of young aspiring preachers – "Are you red hot for Christ?" "Yes, Mr Parr," we would say, shuffling our feet. "Well, it's not enough," he would reply. "You must be *white* hot."

In his later years, when I was a young pastor in Manchester, he asked me to speak to the famous Saturday night crowd in the "old" Bethshan. Being with him in his study beforehand was both exciting and unnerving. He looked at me and said, "What church are *you* from?" "I'm the pastor at Sharon Tabernacle in Moston, Mr Parr," I replied. "Humph . . . and can you preach?" I suffered immediate deprivation of speech and could only stammer something along the lines of doing my best. He then prayed a short rumbling kind of prayer and, as we walked out into the crowded building, said, "Twenty minutes." I preached for twenty minutes and then asked those who wanted to receive Jesus into their lives to raise their hands. The response was remarkable for its non-existence. Mr Parr stood up, paraphrased my message in a few sentences, and told people to repent and trust in Christ. Hands were raised everywhere. It was astonishing. His passion and authority were awesome, almost tangible. As spiritual fathers go he was one of a kind.

We must not, therefore, create a father-figure picture in our minds of a mild and benevolent old gentleman ambling in and out of our lives with a word or two of advice. The impact, even now, of hearing an elderly but vibrant Derek Stone, father to many "sons" in South Africa, calling three hundred leaders to passionate living for Christ in a UK conference[4] in 2002 is still with me: "If you're going to do it, man, do it with heart, all your heart." The sheer passion of his own life inspired us as it lit up his face and filled his voice. The account of the night he rode a Harley Davidson into a youth meeting (something to do with an elderly leader getting youthful attention) was both hilarious and exhilarating. "Men of God have a slipstream," he said. "Get behind those who have passion."

Passions that I encourage

Passion for gospel doctrine – and preaching it

Can anything compare with being arrested, mind, heart, and will, by God's word? Here is the creative and cohesive dynamic of the universe, the sovereign decree of the one true and living God. *"It will not return to me empty,"* He says, *"but will accomplish what I desire and achieve the purpose for which I sent it"* (Isaiah 55:11). Jeremiah knew this. When faced with false critics and constant unbelief, he asked, *"But which of them has stood in the council of the LORD to see or to hear his word?"* (Jeremiah 23:18).

What is our response when, by faith, the word of the Lord passes from the printed page into our understanding? When we begin to "see" how it works, how it holds together, and inter-relates with the divine design and takes its place in the eternal tapestry? But to know that it is in us! That we are called by God to preach and declare it, knowing that as we do God Himself will stand with us and may, by some measureless mystery of grace, touch our minds and lips with holy fire so that, as we speak, we are alive with the word of life.

> *" 'Is not my word like fire,"* declares the LORD, *'and like a hammer that breaks a rock in pieces?' "*   (Jeremiah 23:29)

I know of nothing more glorious and of no time when I am more conscious of the wonders of His love than when His word is alive in me. It seems sometimes as if all other things step back in reverence as the word of the Lord opens a door upon another world, another dimension.

> "Thy words unto my taste are sweet,
> O Lord of hosts, Thy truth I love;
> The light it sheds before my feet,
> Streams from Thy dazzling place above."[5]

Robert Haldane, evangelist and teacher of the early nineteenth century,[6] was made of stern Scottish perseverance and passion. Always concerned to excite and train young men for evangelism and pastoring, and having wrestled through a period of division and disappointment in his church in Scotland, he found his way to Geneva. Little happened and, with his wife, he was preparing to leave when he chanced upon a student in theology who had no understanding whatsoever of Scripture and salvation. Haldane spoke with him and the young man returned bringing other students and friends with him. Though fiercely opposed, the young men, numbering eventually twenty to twenty-five, met for two years with Haldane in his Geneva home as he worked verse by verse, by way of an interpreter, through the Epistle to the Romans. His belief and passion for "the gospel of God" and the sovereignty of grace gripped the small group of students. Many were later to become significant and distinguished spiritual leaders including Merle D'Aubigné (1794– 1872), the Reformation historian, and Adolphe Monod (1802– 56), pastor of the Oratoire Church in Paris and arguably the greatest French preacher of the nineteenth century. Robert Haldane simply did not know, as he gave himself to those young men, what the outcome of his passion would be. He just loved them the best way he knew how, by giving them God's word. Yet how glorious were the consequences.

Spiritual fathers are committed to seeing a new generation of men rise up with the word of the Lord in their hearts and in their mouths. By His word worlds came into being, light burst forth, and life ran like rivers full and free. And when we preach and teach that same word, broken worlds may be restored, light dawn upon the dark surface of the deep, and life arise among the dead. This I know, that the word of God and the Spirit of the sovereign Lord can do this – and we may have passion for both.

Passion for the local church

The church is incredible and wonderful. It is at once the people of God, the body and bride of Christ, the company and community of faith, the dwelling place of the Holy Spirit, and our heavenly Father's family and household. It is the flock of God, the army of the Lord, and the light of the world. In our ministry we cannot afford to entertain secular views of the church because behind those views is a mind completely opposed to God and His purpose – and the church is at the heart of that purpose. There is nothing on earth whatsoever to account for the church: she is divine in origin, composition, and growth. Her great interest is twofold: the Father's kingdom, she being the only body on earth that can see it and the only earthly manifestation of its nature and government; and the Father's Son, her Savior and King, the Lord Jesus Christ, in whose hands all kingdom authority in heaven and on earth presently resides. He is, furthermore, the Bridegroom for whose glorious coming the church bride lovingly and eagerly waits and, while doing so, serves the interests of His kingdom here among the nations of the earth.

The local church is the geographical manifestation of all that the Church is, the Spirit-filled body of Christ through whom He continues to fulfill His Father's will in the world. How utterly and amazingly wonderful this is, and what a costly privilege of grace that we should be members in it and servants of it. At this moment there is a real need for our understanding and vision of the local church to be refreshed and restored. I am persuaded that a significant part of that restoration lies in the hands of today's church fathers as they mentor their spiritual sons.

Passion for people

Just as a passion for the church runs up against the enmity of the natural mind, so too does a passion for people swim against the prevailing tide. Subject to violence, cruelty, abuse, and perversion men, women, and children, made in the image of God, are lost in their own darkness. Holding the tension that calls us to declare both God's anger toward proud sinners and

God's love toward lost wanderers, we also teach the true nature of human beings, their creation as male and female in God's image and their spiritual, social, and physical wholeness constituted to walk in faith and love with the Father in joyful conformity with His perfect and gracious law. Because of our passion for people we are bound to show that sin is the transgression of that law and forfeits all the joys that come from faithful and loving obedience to it.

It is the glory of God's grace that through the Father's passion for people and the Son's submission to the law of the Lord there is eternal hope for humankind. So still, through spiritual fathers and sons by the Spirit, a passion for people burns in the church to inspire compassion, sacrifice, and service. Such a passion must be encouraged to work itself out in creative involvement and dialogue with contemporary issues, i.e. bioethics, existential and post-modern philosophy, syncretism, social structure, and communication. More than just a passing nod to some current areas of concern, a passion for truth, for the historic validity and present authority of the church, the biblical revelation of God and the nature and purpose of man, must be applied with substance and vigor to the discussion by twenty-first-century Christian thinkers, teachers, and prophets.

Passion for God Himself

Supremely it is God who is our passion, God Himself, the triune and eternal God, whose name is holy and whose glory fills the heavens. *"As the deer pants for streams of water,"* whispered David, *"so my soul pants for you, O God"* (Psalm 42:1). Have you wondered why God seemed so often to be kindly disposed toward David, the man of blood? Part of the answer is here. David, underneath all else, had a heart passion for God. He paid dearly and deeply for his sins, but God, who punished him, also knew him, and saw the longing of his heart.

God asks for our hearts (Proverbs 23:26), for them to be filled with love for Him. It is for this reason He has revealed Himself, that we might know Him – and love Him. In the humiliation of Christ, His own dear Son, is revealed the lengths to which He has gone, the terrible depths fathomed and the appalling cup drunk, to make it possible for men and women to love Him.

Fathers know this, that all the record of God's historic revelation of Himself, both in Scripture and in Christ, the saving events and the sacred narrative of them, all the glories of the cross and resurrection, of justification by faith, of sanctification, of kingdom, church, and the life to come, all this and immeasurably more, is to this sovereign and age-long "end," that we might *"draw near to God with a sincere heart in full assurance of faith"* (Hebrews 10:22, my emphasis), and love Him with our whole being – mind, heart, soul, and strength (Luke 10:27). Whatever else the expression "man of God" means, it must mean this, that a man has known and loved the one true and living God.

In mentoring sons it is passion for God, above all else, that we must inspire, and in that I am afraid, for how can I know my heart's affections in such a thing? Preaching passion? Yes. Doctrinal passion? Yes. Church passion? Yes. But with all this and beyond, an abiding love for the infinitely precious and eternal person of God Himself.

> "Lord, it is my chief complaint, that my love is weak and faint,
> Yet I love Thee, and adore; Oh for grace, to love Thee more."[7]

"You who are pastors, may God inflame in you a passion for His centrality and supremacy in your ministry, so that the people you love and serve will say, when you are dead and gone, 'This man knew God. This man loved God. This man lived for the glory of God. This man showed us God week after week. This man, as the apostle said, was "filled with all the fullness of God"' (Ephesians 3:19)."[8]

Notes

1. I do not mean that men of the same quality and caliber will not be seen again, that would not be true. It is that particular group of men with their unique stamp, men who carried the peculiar "stigma" of the classic Pentecostal revival, that will not be seen again.
2. Kenley was a village in the lee of the North Downs in Surrey, England. The Assembly of God Bible School was situated there in beautiful surroundings.
3. It is a remarkable and amusing fact that in churches that would have shunned vestments like the plague, "the vestry" was so significant a place.
4. The Groundlevel Leaders' Conference, Swanwick, Derbyshire, 2002.
5. Harold Horton 1881–1969, *Redemption Hymnal* (1960 ed.), No. 271.

6. Robert Haldane (1764–1842) was converted in 1795 and sold his estate to finance and follow a life of evangelism and missionary endeavor. With his brother James (almost fifty years a preacher in one of their "tabernacles" in Edinburgh), he pioneered a restoration of biblical apostolic Christianity at a time when Scottish Moderate thinking held almost complete sway.
7. William Cowper 1731–1800, *Redemption Tidings* (1960 ed.), No. 397.
8. John Piper, *The Legacy of Sovereign Joy* (IVP, 2000), p. 117.

Chapter 14

Fathers – and Encouragement

Encouragement lies at the heart of fathering:

> *"For you know that we dealt with each of you as a father deals with his own children, encouraging, comforting and urging you to live lives worthy of God, who calls you into his kingdom and glory."* (1 Thessalonians 2:11–12)

Most people appreciate encouragement and thank God for those who are good at giving it. A faithful and cheerful friend can be a wonderful medicine on a blue Monday. A father, too, may encourage us in similar circumstances. In a wider context, however, there are aspects connected with dejection that are different. A father may see as well as a friend that simple encouragement on a "down" day is all that is needed and will be wise enough not to turn such a straightforward remedy into a heavy session (deliver me, Lord, from those who are always wanting to pore over my spiritual entrails). At the same time an encouraging "cheer up, let's go for a coffee" will not do if the blue morning is a symptom of something deeper.

Low spirits or serious dejection

A father *can* be a smile on a dull day, but he is more than that. He is liable to see beneath the surface. If there *is* something more to our discouragement he will find a quiet moment to ask, "OK, what's the trouble?" He is usually able to distinguish between a gloomy face and an aching heart, between temporary low spirits and serious dejection. It is not always easy for others, of course, because we often conceal serious distress behind "I'm alright really" and the "let's go and have a coffee" solution simply aggravates the unperceived distress. A spiritual father rarely makes this mistake. He is more likely to take a second look, size things up, observe without irritating, and refrain from quick answers. He will hold back from immediate assumptions knowing that they risk appearing judgmental, something a more measured approach avoids. Encouragement from this quieter perspective leaves room for the disclosure of feelings and fears unspoken in more animated company.

If we are having more than a miserable morning or a harassed week a true father and mentor will look carefully to identify the cause. As seen already in a previous chapter, he will listen – both to us and to God. If sin is found to be the cause of our unhappiness his encouragement will be tailored to the fact: fathers will never sympathize with sin. Their stance in this respect is a distinguishing mark of their ministry. If they do bring encouragement in such circumstances, it will include careful isolation of the facts and lead to the necessity of appropriate confession and repentance. To be sure, they will stand with us as we do this, and walk with us in the ensuing period of recovery because they know that repentance is both a crisis and a process – it will take time if the repenting is real.

Paul wrote with severity to the believers at Corinth, identifying the sin in their midst, and warning them of its consequences. As an apostle and father he told them clearly what to do (1 Corinthians 5). Paul knew that true fathering demanded that he deal with the sin in the church. Encouragement in this kind of situation will faithfully work through the biblical instruction for the sake of understanding, and carefully work out the biblical procedure for the sake of restoration.

In the context of encouragement these brief paragraphs on seeing beyond the melancholy of a "down" day tend to over-simplify what is often a very difficult process of discovery, discipleship, and restoration. It is enough to say here that if sin is found at the root of our unhappiness true fathering will seek to move us into a framework of confession, repentance, and forgiveness. We will return to look at this again in the next chapter.

When a father's encouragement is particularly needed

When we are weary
We sometimes mistake circumstantial and natural problems for spiritual weakness and inadequacy. The devil will certainly try to maximize such misunderstanding. Spiritual fathers and wise mentors are generally able to see when this is happening – and their perception can be disconcerting. After bewailing our back-slidden condition following a lackluster sermon or some missed prayer session, it is slightly perplexing to have a trusted mentor look at us long and hard and then ask, "Are you sleeping well?" or "When did you last take a break with your wife and family?"

The truth is that zealous and committed leaders (and churches) often drive themselves to the limit, become tired and weary, and need nothing other than rest. It is not a sin to be tired. Some silly zealots actually turn Scripture on its head, do away with the Sabbath, despise rest as sin and attach virtue to being a worn-out wreck. Spiritual fathers are refreshingly normal in this respect and will not mistake the weariness of everyday ministry for backsliding. The devil – and Job's comforters – will be quick to add discouragement to fatigue: "That was really bad ... What a disgrace you are ... Your praying was inadequate and your ministry useless." A true father, however, will ask a few, seemingly irrelevant, questions, take quiet note of various circumstances, and recommend us to see the doctor – after prayer, of course.

When calling is under attack
The call of God lies at the heart of our life and work. By this I mean the specific call of God that sets us aside from all other ambition, desire, and labor, to serve God. This, at one time, was what we described as a call to the ministry and, as said in a previous chapter, I am concerned that both the concept and the expression appear to have fallen out of favor. I wonder why this is? Might it be that the very great doctrine of the priesthood of all believers has been misconstrued and used in an attempt to see all God's people as gift-ministries? Certainly the idea of the called, sent, given, and received pastor, set apart to serve the local church, seems to have slipped out of fashion – and left a void that eldership teams find difficult to fill. Be that as it may,

the call of God remains central to "the ministry." Because of that it is a target for attack. Every called man has known at one time or another the suffocating sense of unhappiness that accompanies the wretched questioning doubt, "Am I really called? Have I imagined it all? How can I be called if this is what I'm like? Perhaps that 'dear brother' is right, I do lack the appropriate skills and will never make it."

Fathers know this miserable frame of mind only too well – they have all been there. They will encourage us with gentle reminders of successful days, of times when God's anointing has rested upon us and our ministry has been wonderfully blessed, of prophetic words that have been given to us, and revelations of truth that have illuminated our minds and hearts.

They will tell us of Abraham's deceitful weaknesses and the cry of Moses, "These people are too much for me;" of David's dribbling "madness" and Elijah's melancholy loneliness after running away from Jezebel; of Jeremiah's reluctance ever to speak again and Jonah's intestinal depression; of Peter's cursing denial and scalding tears – and the glorious preaching that came later; of Paul's aching heart when he recalled what he had been and what he had done before God illuminated the Damascus road; and how unsuitable Mark had seemed to him, until he eventually saw that he was *"profitable to me for the ministry"* (2 Timothy 4:11 KJV).

I am minded, at this moment, to say to you for whom these words are relevant, "Lift your head, look to your Savior, God *did* call you, Christ *has* made you a gift to His body, you *do* have the Holy Spirit." Paul wrote to the Philippian church:

> *"In all my prayers for all of you, I always pray with joy because of your partnership in the gospel from the first day until now, being confident of this, that he who began a good work in you will carry it on to completion until the day of Christ Jesus."*
>
> (Philippians 1:4–6)

Fathers will encourage us to be strong, to persevere through difficult times, to look our fears in the face and declare faith in God. *"Finally,"* said Paul, *"be strong in the Lord and in his mighty power"* (Ephesians 6:10). He went on to specify the armor necessary to make good our position, *"so that when the day of evil comes, you may be able to stand your ground, and after you have done*

everything, to stand" (Ephesians 6:13). God's invariable purpose
for us is conquest through faith.

> *"You then, my son, be strong in the grace that is in Christ Jesus."*
> (2 Timothy 2:1)

When study is dry and prayer lacking

How is it that the great doctrines that were filled a month back
with color and glory can now seem so mundane? All is mono-
chrome and overcast. Why is this? Study seems suddenly so hard
and prayer so empty.

When we share these things with a father he may not
immediately say, "Yes, well it's like this, you need to ... " He
may be strangely laid back about our confession and appear not
to think it terribly serious. The reason for this is probably
twofold: first, he knows that there is a particular kind of "dry
time" that is not unusual, and, second, that most dry times are
not, in fact, sudden occurrences and he does not want to start
digging for reasons straight away.

We may also find that a spiritual father will talk of dry times
positively. "You know, God is not always there for us in the
immediate sense, just waiting upon us. How much do you want
Him? And how will you know how much you want Him if you
never have to seek Him?"

The effort and discipline needed to study and pray through dry
times, simply because faithfulness to our calling requires it, is an
essential part of the Christian ministry. We will never find God
within our own capacity, we are called to search for Him beyond
the limits of our natural skill and ability.

Having said these things, fathers know also that there are
other reasons for dry times, reasons that lie within us. We may
have walked, either deliberately or carelessly, into the wilderness. This is very different from God graciously hiding Himself
from us: this is us foolishly, even sinfully, hiding ourselves from
Him. A faithful father will bring us to the truth of the matter –
even if it hurts.

When little seems to be happening in the church

Early on in our ministry in Maidstone things were somewhat
difficult, little was happening, and response was low. I so much
wanted the touch of God upon my preaching, but the more I

tried the harder it all seemed. In those days it was the custom at the close of Sunday services for the minister to stand at the door and shake hands with the people as they were leaving. On one Sunday morning when I had preached as best I knew how, a visitor, a small elderly man dressed in a black suit, shook my hand at the door. And then, with a twinkle of seriousness in his eye, he looked directly at me and said quietly, "Conserve your strength, young man, conserve your strength." His direct look lingered for a moment, and then he was gone. The impression upon me was profound, for I knew, immediately and exactly, what he meant. I was trying too hard. There was a lack of faith in my ministry for which I was trying to compensate with effort and "zeal." In the attempt I was straining, strident, and intense.

Who was the man? I have no idea. Over the years I have watched for him (I would know him immediately) for he spoke God's word to me. Just one sentence, but I have never forgotten it.

When little seems to be happening in the church, do not strain at it, conserve your strength. Extremity of effort will not bring blessing.

When criticism is biting

Not all criticism "bites." In fact some criticism is really quite good for us. Those attached to us are sometimes afraid to tell us home truths; others have no such scruples. Fathers will often advise us to listen to some critics: "What is your response to that? Do they have a point? Could there be some truth in what he is saying?"

But other criticism, scandalous criticism, does "bite;" it is often unjust, destructive, or libelous, and can cause deep pain. Spiritual fathers can usually tell the difference. They will listen to, and feel, our hurt, identify the malevolent spirit behind it, assure us of our standing in God's grace and call, and pray with us as we resist the falsehood.

The truth is, we are going to be criticized, and it is going to be unpleasant. Although large crowds *"listened to him with delight"* (Mark 12:37), Jesus never made popularity a mark of spiritual success. The spirit of the world system is opposed to God and will oppose those born of His spirit. *"If the world hates you,"* Jesus said, *"keep in mind that it hated me first"* (John 15:18). We must do as He says – and accept that even in churches people may be motivated by the spirit of the world. All of this is true. Joseph suffered it, as did Moses, Joshua, Samuel, David, Jeremiah, Daniel, and Paul, to name but some of the scandalized servants of the Lord.

But there is another truth, immeasurably greater. There is nothing formed against us that cannot, through submission, be made to serve God's glory in our lives. True fathers will not just comfort and reassure us, they will remind us that we cultivate character by the way we react to obstacles, persecution, and scandal.

There is a kingdom principle behind the process. It is this:

> *"Woe to you when all men speak well of you,*
>   *for that is how their fathers treated the false prophets.*
>
> *But I tell you who hear me:* **Love** *your enemies,* **do good** *to those who hate you,* **bless** *those who curse you,* **pray** *for those who ill-treat you."*   (Luke 6:26–28, my emphasis)

In other words, we are to face negative action with positive reaction, not aggressively but with faith-filled humility, because God works the process for our good, to strengthen our resolve and build up our faith.

> *"We know that in all things God works for the good of those who love him, who have been called according to his purpose. For those God foreknew he also predestined to be conformed to the likeness of his Son, that he might be the firstborn among many brothers. And those he predestined, he also called; those he called, he also justified; those he justified, he also glorified. What, then, shall we say in response to this? If God is for us, who can be against us?"*
>   (Romans 8:28–31)

The process or road by which we are conformed to the likeness of the Father's Son is beset with those battles in which we overcome *un*godliness. God's predestined purposes for us will therefore include rejection, contradiction, and scandal, but also justification, sanctification, and glory: it is the royal road. This is why the spiritual fathers of every age call us to *"consider him who endured such opposition from sinful men, so that you will not grow weary and lose heart"* (Hebrews 12:3).[1] Considering Christ, thinking long on Him and His life, meditating upon His love, and contemplating His sacrifice will reduce anger and melt self-pity clean away.

When we have made a mistake

There is a corner of the evangelical field that is very unattractive. It is inhabited by people who appear to make no mistakes, who seem to have arrived at doctrinal perfection, and have appointed themselves scrutinizers of everyone else. If you have made a mistake do not go there (in fact do not go there at all).

Ministers make mistakes. So do fathers and mentors. Mistakes do not qualify us for ministry (the idea that you cannot help someone in trouble unless you have been in the same trouble yourself is very dangerous), rather they demonstrate our fallibility and need of grace.

Spiritual fathers will encourage us to admit and face up to mistakes, and where appropriate apologize, whether to an individual, a group, or the church. They will also want to look at the circumstances surrounding the mistake, our thinking (or lack of it), and anything that predisposes us to make the same kind of error again. "Do you think," he may say, "that you have a weakness here? That you lose your patience too quickly, that you speak without sufficient thought?" Too many mistakes along certain lines, administrative, relational, procedural, pastoral, indicate a need for fatherly assessment and mentoring.

Simple encouragement, in all these things, is a gift, a blessed ability to light upon the tired smile hiding in a cloud of frowns. My colleague Derek Savage, a faithful friend to many leaders and churches, has the gift. I have seen a room full of weary ministers suddenly quicken into life at his entry, like a gloomy corner touched by a ray of sunshine. His very fine preaching is the same. No wonder leaders and churches love and welcome him. In ministry, even when handling difficult issues and expounding strong passages, Derek still retains the encouraging note. He's good to be with.

Some find the negatives all too easily. It leads, oftentimes, to being surrounded by others of a similar stamp. We have all overheard at some time conversations similar to this:

"Hello, dear brother. It's been difficult this week, as, of course, it was last week, and we can expect it to be the same next week. The work of God in a hostile world is a hard business."

"Yes, dear brother, I find it the same. 'Through much tribulation ...'"

"Yes, this vale of tears and woe ... Did you know that so and so has fallen into sin? Yes, another one. I myself fight daily with beasts at Ephesus. Death and decay in all around I see ... How about you?"

"Yes. We too have woodworm. It's all these new songs. Why can't we have the old ones?"

"Did you have a particular one in mind?"

"Yes, though my memory isn't what it was, and my heart and flesh is failing ..."

"What was it, dear brother?"

"'There is joy in serving Jesus, as I journey on my way.'"

"O deep joy."

In the New Testament Barnabas is the great encourager. His name means "son of consolation." It should not be thought, however, that such a person is meek and kindly to the point of weak mildness. Barnabas faced up to Paul over the suitability of John Mark and eventually parted company with him on the matter. He was a strong man. Encouragement from a weak man lacks conviction, from a strong man it carries worth. Whatever the rights and wrongs of the Mark incident, there was at least consolation for him in the support of Barnabas.[2]

Fathers encourage us...

- *By listening to our longings, looking at our plans and strategies, and affirming our enthusiasm.* Sometimes our peers do not always engage with our plans and strategies, they just want to tell us of their own! But fathers will listen with pleasure to the desires and designs of their sons, and share their expectations with real interest.

- *By asking for our opinions, giving value to our views, and noting with care what we think.* I can still recall the glow of pleasure when I was asked, as a young minister, for my thinking on a particular issue by an older and highly respected leader. My ideas were not at all new to him, but he was genuinely interested in the development of my thought.

- *By unwinding in our company, showing interest in our natural pursuits and relaxing with us.* Fathers know that most men need a mental and physical outlet for their energies. Super-spirituality may frown on this but we do well to remember that Jesus Himself rested with His disciples, and that true spirituality is much more than an unbroken round of religious duties and exercises.

- *By knowing wife and family, inquiring after their welfare, and listening with attention as we talk about them.* Simple experience tells fathers that home-life, parenting, holidays, education, health – all the interests and concerns of everyday life – lie close to the surface. If things are strained here, they tend to be strained everywhere. A father will not miss that.[3]

- *By recognizing hard work, commending it, and affirming the dedicated use of time and energy.* If faithful labor is to be commended and rewarded at Christ's return – *"Well done, good and faithful servant"* (Matthew 25:23) – then we may also recognize it now. It is one of the great joys of fathering to commend a son's endeavors. "Children need encouragement often more than admonition, to have their good behavior commended as much as their bad behavior rebuked. Fathers are not to 'provoke' their children, lest they become discouraged, Colossians 3:21."[4]

- *By identifying strengths, urging positive thought, speech, and action, and cheering us on.* Spiritual fathers and mentors are affirming rather than doubting: "I'm sure you can do it, you have the courage and the skill. Go for it, do your best, don't stop, press on. By God's grace you can do it. You *can* do it!"

Notes

1. There is an excellent chapter on coping with criticism in Tom Marshall's book *Understanding Leadership* (Sovereign World, 1996).
2. Notwithstanding the family connection, which may have had some bearing on the dispute.
3. Of course, with single leaders these particular considerations will not apply, but there are others that will.
4. John Stott, *The Preacher's Portrait* (The Tyndale Press, 1961), p. 81.

Chapter 15

Fathers – and the Flaws and Failures

This is more difficult than the issues already handled. Spiritual fathers find themselves talking through a wide cross section of life and ministry issues – marriage relationships, family life, parenting, vision, doctrine, church problems, peer pressure, manners, and more. A serious character flaw, an ongoing failure of some kind, is different. Most life and ministry issues are a matter of understanding, experience, self-discipline, and development, and are usually public or personal. A serious flaw is rarely public or even personal; it is generally concealed in the private life, hidden away in some dark and secret corner. Close friends rarely know of it, and the same is often true, sadly, of wife and family. This is why, if the flaw or failure comes to light, people say, "I never had the slightest idea," "I simply can't believe it," "How can you live with someone and not know?"

We are probably thinking already of moral flaws and failures. Unhappily they are not uncommon and more leaders are struggling with them privately on a regular basis than we may care to admit. The tide of illicit sexuality is at high water mark in our culture. Shameful inclinations can be indulged on the Web in the "safety" of home, and the warnings of Scripture (strong passages in almost every epistle) regarding worldliness, loose sexual behavior, and impurity are too rarely the subject of contemporary preaching and teaching. These warnings, however, are there for our good. They are God's gracious "No Trespassing" signs. When we circumnavigate them, together with His censures on crude language, worldly pleasures, and immodest dress, the vital sense of awe and fear regarding Him is lost – and it is the fear of the Lord that is the beginning of wisdom. There is a price to pay for these things falling prey to the legalistic tyranny of liberty, evangelical "correctness," and user-friendly church. Part of the price is the number of leaders who secretly wrestle with sexual habits and failures, who too often find themselves ministering publicly while carrying a bleeding wound privately, and an increase in those being discovered.

Slow to anger

It seems that spiritual fathers are more likely to find themselves hearing confession regarding moral temptation than ministerial colleagues, elders, or wives. Why would this be so? Mainly, I think, because spiritual fathers tend not to stand so close to us as family and friends, are not usually part of our everyday life, and may not therefore react immediately and emotionally to a major problem. One of the lovely things about God is the slowness of His anger. Fathers tend to "image" Him in this respect. The anger of a wife or child or even of a close friend at the disclosure of fault or failure in a loved one often follows swiftly upon the shock of discovery. It is not only the nature of the sin itself that is so shocking but the deceit employed in order to indulge it and the betrayal involved. A natural father might feel this sense of betrayal more quickly than a spiritual father, though slowness to anger does not mean absence of anger. Slowness to anger gives room for conversation and may mean that the offender does not feel immediately cut off, that there is space in which to talk. Nevertheless, slow anger may be more real at the last, being considered and true rather than reactionary and emotional.

Fathers cannot sympathize with sin. None of us can, especially in ourselves. Yet we are all prone to do so because we feel there is "understanding" in it. In those spiritual sons of mine that have fallen, a common thread, among others, has been their desire for me to understand and sympathize. Almost every conversation, text message, letter, and email has had this note in it: "Please understand me, I couldn't help it, it just happened." Sadly, sin, whether we are taken "unawares" (and I am never too sure about that) or caught in the process of deceit, is a deadly "element:" it cannot be accommodated. The only possible response is confession and repentance.

But what then? What of restitution, receiving forgiveness, and restoration? For fathers and mentors, and, I think, for teams and churches as a whole, there is more to learn.

I fear that we are not so good as we could be at walking with those who are in confession and repentance, not good at helping them to face their failure, sit beneath Scripture's judgment of it, and deal with the details. I am not talking about those who are unabashed, who excuse their sin and continue in it, but those who are convicted and ashamed, and are seeking true repentance. And there is the point. Repentance does have to be sought. In this regard I suspect that spiritual fathers are the best people to walk with those who are truly searching. It is not the words of repentance that are the problem initially: they often come tumbling out. It is the change of mind, the adjustment of will, and the necessary restitution that invests the initial words with ongoing action (and that will eventually embrace forgiveness) that is the more difficult. It is this that takes the time, love, and patience – and is sometimes misunderstood.[1]

While, therefore, fathers will not accommodate sin in a disciple, they are peculiarly fitted to serve in the process of repentance and restoration.

Sooner or later, in long-lasting relationships, the tendency towards fault or failure along certain lines becomes apparent. It is not often spoken about between colleagues, usually because they fear that to do so would damage their attachment. In these circumstances a true spiritual father is of great value. A leader may feel free to talk to him about a colleague, to voice fears regarding a defect or flaw that is not being addressed, a trend that may be developing into a crisis. A spiritual father will know how to hear such fears, and how to deal with the issue itself, particularly if he is accepted by the team as a whole.

Flaws need to be faced. The writer to the Hebrews referred to them as *"everything that hinders and the sin that so easily entangles ... "* (Hebrews 12:1). Fathers can help us to look at ourselves. They are aware of the inclination in those who have lived with a flaw for a long time of justifying and accepting it instead of "throwing it off." Practical suggestions and help with the "throwing off" process will be needed, monitoring as well as mentoring therefore, with large supplies of grace for good measure. I am sure, in circumstances like this, that fathering among sons is preferable to "vulnerability sessions" among colleagues. They are often too open, too rough, and tend to exposure without remedy.

With a sin committed it is different. We are bound to speak to a colleague or friend in such circumstances quickly. That would be the counsel of all spiritual fathers.

Note

1. In looking at how we father the repenting offender, there is real need to look also at how we father those offended, many of whom come to the desperately unhappy conclusion that they are the ones to blame.

Chapter 16

Fathers – and Personal Spirituality

We said in an earlier chapter that spiritual fathers serve the interests of our inner life, seeking to ensure that there is a true and consistent measure of God's fullness in us. That they do this, inevitably, out of the reality of their own inner life constitutes a very great challenge. I seriously doubt that any leader will function as a father in Christ who does not carry the wounds of a deep and private battle over self and supremacy.

Spirituality is not merely the wearing of a certain kind of demeanor, the acquiring of various kindly attributes or a self-effacing reserve. At the heart of it lies a bruising struggle. There is in all of us an "I" that is possessed of a terrible insistence to dominate. This is the point of issue and unless we surrender here and allow the nature of Christ to overcome us we will lack spirituality in depth. And if we lack it there, in principle, we will lack it everywhere in practice. This is true for all believers but, I suspect, the struggle is most acute in those called by God and given by Christ as gift-ministries.

Abraham, father of all the faithful, faced it during the worst night of his life, when, after many years of rest with the laughter of the precious Isaac filling his tent and his life, a battle from long ago had to be fought again over the throne of his heart (Genesis 22:1–3). By morning Abraham had surrendered – and won. God, and faith in Him, was central still. But the struggle tore Abraham to the roots. From that dark night, so far as he was concerned, Isaac, his beloved son, was as good as dead (Hebrews 11:19). He had put him to death in his heart.

We stand, here, at the heart of our father and son thinking. The shadow of the crucifixion cast its long finger back to touch the heart of Abraham with its aching agony. And it reaches forward through the rolling years to touch the hearts of a myriad fathers with the same anguish.

> *"He grew up before him like a tender shoot ...*
> *Yet it was the Lord's will to crush him and cause him to*
> *suffer ... "* (Isaiah 53:2, 10)

The crucified life

Spirituality, for us, must always come the way of death because there is that in us which only "death" can deal with. Paul teaches clearly that we were "crucified with Christ" in what some call the "positional" sense:

> *"I have been crucified with Christ and I no longer live, but Christ*
> *lives in me."* (Galatians 2:20)

By "positional" is meant that our "crucifixion" took place by reason of our union with Christ, that we were "in Him" positionally, so that what happened to Him is said to have happened to us also. When I was at school it was the custom for the headmaster at Monday morning assembly to announce that on Saturday "we" had played such and such a school at some sports fixture. If "we" had won there was much cheering because, although the team had done the playing, we were all deemed to have been "in" the team, so "we" had won. In some similar sense God has included us all "in Christ," an expression used constantly by the apostle Paul to show that His life is our life, His death our death, His resurrection our resurrection, and His victory our victory ("we" won). Paul exclaims,

> *"If we have been united with him like this in his death, we will*
> *certainly also be united with him in his resurrection."*
> (Romans 6:5)

What a blessed "certainly!" The concept (which, while admittedly difficult, is so clearly declared) lies behind the wonderful passage in Ephesians 2:4–7,

> *"But because of his great love for us, God, who is rich in*
> *mercy, made us alive with Christ even when we were dead in*

transgressions – it is by grace you have been saved. And God raised us up with Christ and seated us with him in the heavenly realms in Christ Jesus, in order that in the coming ages he might show the incomparable riches of his grace, expressed in his kindness to us in Christ Jesus."

Charles Wesley saw it and wrote:

"Soar we now where Christ has led,
Following our exalted Head;
Made like Him, like Him we rise,
Ours the cross, the grave, the skies!"

This massive and incredible doctrine of union with Christ, of which the teaching of a crucified life is an integral part, is a major and fundamental element in the scheme of salvation. Because we are joined in union with Christ we died when He died:

"Those who belong to Christ Jesus have crucified the sinful nature with its passions and desires." (Galatians 5:24)

"May I never boast except in the cross of our Lord Jesus Christ, through which the world has been crucified to me, and I to the world." (Galatians 6:14)

Underlying the cultivation of the spiritual life therefore, dealing with what Paul calls the *"passions and desires"* of the sinful nature and *"the world,"* is this doctrine of union with Christ. How we deal practically, now, in our daily living, with the sinful nature and the world will depend very much on what we believe happened in that death. Has *"the world been crucified to me"*? Is the sinful nature *"with its passions and desires"* crucified for those who belong to Christ Jesus? If that is the position in which we are placed by Christ's death, so far as the sinful nature and the world is concerned, then we must reckon from that position when faced with sin and temptation. It is this very thing that Paul teaches in Romans 6:6–7:

"For we know that our old self was crucified with him so that the body of sin might be done away with, that we should no longer be slaves to sin – because anyone who has died has been freed from sin."

Spiritual fathers and mentors know that this is the doctrinal ground out of which the fragrant blooms of the spiritual life grow. The distinctive marks and characteristics of that life are not unknown, but the soil from which they draw their strength and beauty may be less familiar. And here is the difficulty. If we constantly call for the blossom and the fruit, for the sweet savor and taste of the spiritual life, without attending to the ground and soil in which it lives and from which it grows, we will excite frustration to start with and create imitation at the last – and bring spirituality into derision among the very people who should love and value it best.[1]

True fatherhood and mentoring has much to do here. The spiritual life, rooted in union with Christ, faces a popular Christian world fascinated by self-esteem, self-realization, and the personal feel-good factor. The apostle Paul's longing after God, *"I want to know Christ and the power of his resurrection,"* is followed by *"the fellowship of sharing in his sufferings, becoming like him in his death"* and rises to, *"and so, somehow, to attain to the resurrection from the dead"* (Philippians 3:10–11).

He knew he had not taken hold of it, but the soaring trumpet note of spiritual valor rose up out of the sounding chords and harmonies of theology and history to sound along the rolling years and call his spiritual sons to the pursuit of God:

> *"Brothers, I do not consider myself yet to have taken hold of it. But one thing I do: Forgetting what is behind and straining towards what is ahead, I press on towards the goal to win the prize for which God has called me heavenwards in Christ Jesus."*
> (Philippians 3:13–14)

Note

1. Why is union with Christ so little preached and taught? If we think it to be out of date or in some way old fashioned and irrelevant I suggest that we be ashamed and review with humility our understanding of the gospel of God. Are there no apostles and teachers now who will take such truths and bring them to God's people afresh? I am sure there are and we must encourage them. This is not out of date. This is not the theological meanderings of a long lost age. This is truth! This is for today because it is for everyday.

Chapter 17

When Fathers Hurt

I am always moved whenever the words of David, King of Israel, come to mind,

> *"O my son Absalom! My son, my son Absalom! If only I had died instead of you – O Absalom, my son, my son!"*
>
> (2 Samuel 18:33)

His voice is filled with the anguish of a broken heart. When I read the words the years seem somehow to slip away and David's cry becomes the echo of a thousand aching hearts as fathers weep over wayward sons. The warrior king with a heart full of poetry and song – an emotive combination of majesty and music – lifted his heartbreak to heaven and could not be comforted.

Fathers are not able to avoid being hurt. A teacher will be frustrated at the failure of a scholar, a master disappointed at the defection of a disciple, but a father will cry over the loss of a son. I am aware that David's grief over Absalom was severely censured by Joab, and that the censure was not wholly undeserved. Some of David's anguish came from the knowledge that he might have handled the young man better, but the heartbreak was real for all that. There are few of us for whom hindsight has no lesson. And if love lies at the heart of fathering, then fathers will be hurt. It's the loving heart, the heart that cares, cherishes, and hopes, that runs the risk of being broken.

Backsliding breaks the heart...

Backsliding is not mentioned so much today. Unbalanced doctrines of grace have made it easy to live casually and carelessly without conviction. No matter how we may behave, shame is deemed inappropriate, and feelings of guilt viewed as well nigh heretical. True spiritual fathers have too much biblical sense in the face of such flawed doctrine and will not allow misbehavior to hide behind easy pretexts such as, "God understands, His grace covers me and His love is unconditional."

Leaders do backslide. Familiarity with spiritual things can make us careless while notions born of positive thinking supported by natural talent are liable to undervalue (if not view with faint derision) the disciplines of private prayer and personal communion. Sadly, hiding a cold heart, at least for a while, is not that difficult. Spiritual fathers, however, have an "ability" somehow to sense and detect it, particularly if the relationship is on a regular basis. *"Demas has deserted me,"* wrote Paul (2 Timothy 4:10), but I have little doubt that the apostle sensed the decline and desertion in the heart of Demas before the actual act of leaving took place. "Knowing" that something is wrong is an element in fathering not easy to define.

Being part of a leadership team is not an automatic means of spiritual reality. We may backslide at the heart of such a team, and deceive our closest colleagues and friends. The heady excitement of spiritual planning, prophetic vision, and evangelistic strategy can hide a dry and empty life. I've heard too many good men say, "We walked and worked together for a long time, but nobody knew ..." Sometimes we can love our brothers to the point where we simply will not believe that there might be a problem; in this case the love has become sentimental and the relationship counter-productive.

On a worship team it can be the same. The broken threads of private devotion can lie concealed behind the laughter of a team meeting, behind the rhythm of praise and worship. The harmony of the choir can hide a lukewarm heart and a bleak spirit. The high-powered strategist or the dreaming poet will not always see it, but the father often will. Feet on the ground with mind and heart engaged, he hears the emptiness in the multitude of words and the straining note in the endless songs.

"Grief is the price we pay for love"

Sometimes there is nothing more you can say or do. The care, the counsel, the gentleness, the firmness, all seems hopeless. You watch a "child" walk away and you keep calm, but inside you ache and hurt with desperation. At such times we are learning a deep and painful truth: love does not initially guarantee a son or a daughter's compliance. As Queen Elizabeth wrote to the New York memorial service after September 11, "Grief is the price we pay for love." Paul's words in 1 Corinthians 13:8, *"Love never fails,"* do not mean love always works immediately but that it always works eventually. Love is not a formula for getting what we want; it's an attitude of heart that reaches into the ages beyond initial rejection:

> *"Having loved his own who were in the world, he now showed them the full extent of his love."* (John 13:1)

Fathers may work together with other leaders to help a fallen friend, with counsel and structure for restitution, if accepted. Going many extra miles is part of a father's heart. Yet when all has been said and done it may be to no avail. The temptation is to chase, ring, engineer "spontaneous" meetings, organize prayer nights, send a stream of notes, leave messages on mobiles, but at some point we have to stand still before God, and put it all down. I only really learned what "giving it to God" meant when I lost a spiritual "son" and couldn't get him back. How can we just let them go? I can only say that "giving to God" sounds better than letting him go. But it still hurts.

Rejection

The apostle Paul knew the very deep unhappiness occasioned by spiritual children turning their back on their fathers in Christ. The Corinthians, whom Paul called his children on three separate occasions, questioned his ministry (2 Corinthians 10:10), threw doubt upon his apostleship (2 Corinthians 11:5–6), compared him unfavorably to other apostles (2 Corinthians 12:11–13), and demanded proof of his authority (2 Corinthians 13:3), when they themselves were the proof (2 Corinthians 3:2–3). Their shameful attitude drove Paul to defend himself in uncharacteristic terms. All of this on top of the distress he felt at their quarrelling and division, their toleration of grievous immorality, and their abuse of the Lord's Supper and spiritual gifts. Because they were his spiritual children their worldliness and sin reflected upon him. He must have felt it. His sorrow at their immature weakness was surely mixed with feelings of shame and doubt regarding his ministry to them.

We have to reach back into the life of Moses to find a similar anguish of heart in a spiritual father. The sin of the people he was leading affected him deeply. He told the people:

> *" 'You have committed a great sin. But now I will go up to the LORD; perhaps I can make atonement for your sin.' So Moses went back to the LORD and said, 'Oh, what a great sin these people have committed! They have made themselves gods of gold. But now, please forgive their sin – but if not, then blot me out of the book you have written.' "*
> (Exodus 32:30–32)

Moses felt himself so involved and identified with the sin of the people that any punishment for them he considered his own.

All spiritual fathers know the hurt of rejection, of being criticized or ignored. Charles Haddon Spurgeon (1834–92), the Victorian "Prince of Preachers" and father to a multitude of students and pastors in his remarkable lifetime, lived to hear his name and doctrine (by the preaching of which so many of them had come to Christ) criticized and denounced by many of those very pastors. At his resignation from the Baptist Union in 1887 over the downgrade issue,[1] a censure was passed upon him by many of those same men that has never been rescinded. "The fight is killing me," he said in 1891 as he left London for Mentone for the last time.

Fathers also have to live with their own mistakes – and that hurts too. It simply is not possible to get it right every time. There is a difference, however, in making a genuine mistake, for which we may ask pardon, and deliberately maintaining a wrong course of action.

For Eli, the priest of God, there was no glad ending. Though the young Samuel heard the voice of the Lord, the child of the Temple was no son of the priest. Eli's sons were wild libertines who disgraced their father and brought him to anguish and death. But much of the fault was his own. The words spoken to Samuel regarding Eli were terrible in the extreme:

> *"For I told him that I would judge his family for ever because of the sin he knew about; his sons made themselves contemptible, and he failed to restrain them."*
> (1 Samuel 3:13; see also 1 Samuel 2:22–25)

There is a very real responsibility upon fathers. They are bound to speak the truth to their sons, and to do so early, so that their later words will be heard with respect. Currently biblical teaching on headship has, unhappily and dangerously I believe, been diverted into an ongoing controversy regarding women in leadership. Divine authority and headship with spiritual authority and paternal responsibility have fallen among thieves and been stripped of their raiment. There is still ministry. There was with Eli, *"He had led Israel for forty years"* (1 Samuel 4:18), but the ministry lacked authority. Subsequently the ark of God was stolen and the glory of God departed. Everyone and everything, both in the Church and in the world, is affected adversely when God's order is neglected or interfered with and fathers fail to fulfill their place and responsibility.

Note

1. Spurgeon's expression, "We are going downhill at breakneck speed," to describe the descent into theological liberalism in the latter half of the nineteenth century in England, gave the name "The Down-Grade" to the trend. The Down-Grade was committed to a broad and liberal view of Scripture supported by higher critical views with a corresponding denial of evangelical supernaturalism, and, in Spurgeon's particular case, evangelical Calvinism.

Chapter 18

A Father's Joy

The overflow of the Father's heavenly joy, *"This is my Son, whom I love; with him I am well pleased"* (Matthew 3:17), lies as a divine foundation for the joys and pleasures of all fathering. There is great pleasure in the character formed. The same words are used again in the later episode at Jesus' transfiguration (Matthew 17:5), as once again the Father expresses his delight – *"This is my Son, whom I love; with him I am well pleased."* But here there is an instruction added, *"Listen to him!"*

The Father's pleasure in His Son's character, therefore, also looked forward to the Son's work and ministry. The truth is that a father's joy in his son always anticipates that for which his fathering has prepared him. He knows that ministry will be an inevitable combination of conflict and victory, but that in order to win through he dare not shield him from it, that loving obedience worked into the character by faith will carry the day. A wise father knows all this but will not inherit the joy unless he allows the son to go.

Abraham somehow sensed it with Isaac, and the prodigal's father knew it with anguish as he watched his son close the gate behind him. But all pales into insignificance as the Father of all the ages released His Son to a dark, dying world. To Nazareth, obscurity, innocence (for innocence is perfection untested), and the long lonely years of obedience learned through suffering. Then to a brief ministry ending in betrayal, death, and heart-breaking alone-ness. What, in all the eternal Godhead, sustained the Father and the Son in such a venture? It seems a colossal impertinence to even think about it leave alone comment upon it, but the Son Himself declared that *"God so loved the world that He gave . . . "* It was this wondering realization of His place at the heart of the Father's love for the world that gave Him joy and sustained His resolve. And that joy in the midst of darkness and death gazed with faith into the dawning day of an age to come at a greater and deeper joy, to a glory that was His before the world began, so that it is said of Him in Hebrews 12:2, *"who for the joy set before Him endured the cross, scorning its shame, and sat down at the right hand of the throne of God"* (my emphasis).

However, the joy of restoration to that magnificent glory in the age to come shone with a brilliance much greater than its shining in the age that was gone (if we can talk of the eternal procession of the ages in such a way). Why was this? Because in the age that was past the glory was that of Father and Son by the Spirit. But in the age to come the Son saw that glory, the glory of the image and likeness of God, upon a *"multitude that no one could count"* (Revelation 7:9) for He, the Son, is now *"bringing many sons to glory"* (Hebrews 2:10). The Father's joy is in His beloved Son bringing back many sons, and the Son's joy is in doing His Father's will. It was fitting, therefore,

> *"that God, for whom and through whom everything exists, should make the author of their salvation perfect through suffering. Both the One who makes men holy and those who are made holy are of **the same family**. So Jesus is not ashamed to call them brothers. He says,*
>
> > *'I will declare your name to my brothers;*
> >   *in the presence of the congregation I will sing your*
> >   *praises.'"*
>
> (Hebrews 2:10–12, my emphasis)

Here is the joy of fatherhood and sonship, a joy that cannot be without the pain of release and the anguish of forsakenness; a joy that embraces the heartache now, the battle today, for the greater joy tomorrow. There will be sacrifice and death. Fathers and sons will know and feel it, and it is a denial of all that the Christian faith reveals to say otherwise or suggest another way – that surely, is the work of the devil who set before Jesus wealth, wonders, and worship in the here and now. It was a poor alternative to suffering, death, resurrection, and glory to come – *and the joy of having every son back home in the Father's house.*

It is every father's joy now to show his sons the royal road to that glory and joy, the road of temptation, overcoming, endurance and grace, and to encourage in every proper way the life of faith, obedience, and love.

> *"For what is our hope, our joy, or the crown in which we will glory in the presence of our Lord Jesus when he comes? Is it not you? Indeed, you are our glory and joy."* (1 Thessalonians 2:19–20)

We are not hirelings, paper tigers, empty talkers. We are fathers and sons, soldiers and saints. Called to endure the dark night, despise the hurt and pain, and sing the warrior psalm. We have a vision of a new day, another age, a better world, a sweeter song, a kingdom that will never pass away – and the Lamb upon His throne.

> *"For as in Adam all die, so in Christ all will be made alive ... Then the end will come, when he hands over the kingdom to* **God the Father** *after he has destroyed all dominion, authority, and power. For he must reign until he has put all his enemies under his feet. The last enemy to be destroyed is death ... When he has done this, then* **the Son himself** *will be made subject to him who put everything under him, so that God may be all in all."*
> (1 Corinthians 15:22, 24–26, 28, my emphasis)

And a father's final word

> *"Therefore, my dear brothers, stand firm. Let nothing move you. Always give yourselves fully to the work of the Lord, because you know that your labor in the Lord is not in vain."*
> (1 Corinthians 15:58)